⊕ An Observer's

Home Built
Shelves, Cupboards and Containers

E.. ... J PLAYGROUP
ATHERTON STREET,
ST. HELENS
TEL. 25528

CU00982983

HOME BUILT
Shelves, Cupboards and Containers

Walter Burnett

Line drawings by Walter Burnett and R. F. Fraser

FREDERICK WARNE

Published by Frederick Warne (Publishers) Ltd, London, 1983

Text © Walter Burnett 1983
Parts 1–3 illustrations © Walter Burnett 1983

Appendix illustrations © Frederick Warne (Publishers) Ltd, 1983

ISBN 0 7232 2955 4

Filmset and printed in Great Britain by
BAS Printers Limited, Over Wallop, Hampshire

Contents

                                                                    Page

Introduction   7

Part 1: Ready-made storage containers   9
Adapting ready-made wooden containers: tea chests; altering tea chests. Using other ready-made wooden containers. Adapting ready-made non-wooden containers: cardboard and fibre boxes; cardboard and fibre drums and cylinders
Further ideas for ready-made containers: 'modular' wall storage units; wooden containers adapted to make dining/work table and seats

Part 2: Purpose-made storage containers   33
Making a hinged-lid box in coated chipboard. Making a hinged-lid box in plywood
Further ideas for purpose-made containers: bedding box; storage/coffee table/seating; desk; filing boxes; display case

Part 3: Shelving   45
Using existing side-supports. Fixing shelving against walls. Fixing adjustable shelf systems to a wall. Free-standing shelves. Designing shelves. The options: solid- or open-sided shelves. Constructing solid-sided shelves. Turning shelves into cupboards. Ladder-sided shelves
Further ideas for shelving: alcove storage units; shelves; wardrobe/dressing-table arrangement; cleaning/household materials storage; wardrobe/suitcase/shoes storage

Appendix 1 Tools and equipment   70

Appendix 2 Measurements, squareness and marking out   78

Appendix 3 Wood, panelling and boards   83

Appendix 4 Screws and nails   87

Appendix 5 Adhesives   91

Appendix 6 Painting and finishing   92

Appendix 7 Hinges, fittings and accessories   97

Appendix 8 Wall fixings   107

Appendix 9 Storage box seating   111

Introduction

It is said that if you *give* a man a fish you feed him for a day, whereas if you *teach* him to fish you feed him for life.

This book has been planned and written with this saying very much in mind. Rather than present detailed blow-by-hammer-blow accounts of the construction of smart pieces of furniture, which are probably not what the reader wants to make anyway, it concentrates on broad ideas, and on providing guidance on the techniques necessary to fulfil the reader's *own* design requirements.

The storage possibilities in ready-made and purpose-made containers are reviewed, to show how the former can be adapted for home use, and how the latter can be planned or designed for maximum economy and ease of construction.

The book is divided into four sections: the first three dealing with materials and ideas, the fourth consisting of a series of Appendices covering tools, fittings and techniques common to the first three sections. These Appendices have been placed at the end of the book, not because they are optional reading, but to avoid repetition and digressions in the text. In many cases the information in the Appendices is vital, particularly to newcomers to woodworking and allied techniques. Generally, where a tool, technique or material is mentioned in the text, a bracketed note refers the reader to the appropriate Appendix on the *first mention* only.

Throughout the book measurements are given in millimetres followed by the nearest *practical* Imperial equivalent. These practical equivalents are not exact, for instance 12 mm is *nearly* ½ inch, or 47 hundredths of an inch. Such conversions are cumbersome, and difficult (if not impossible!) for the homeworker to measure accurately. Having chosen either the metric or Imperial system, always stick to it throughout the design and construction of the project. Changing from one system to the other can only lead to inaccuracy or mistakes.

Part 1

Ready-made storage containers

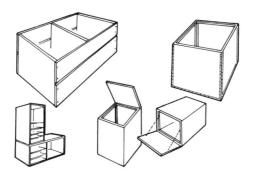

Part 1
Ready-made storage containers

Adapting ready-made wooden containers

The wide variety of containers which can be adapted to provide storage facilities in the home is one of the happier aspects of mass packaging and international transportation.

Despite the protests from ecologists, timber is still widely used in packaging. Fruit trays, apple and orange boxes are readily available from greengrocers and supermarkets. Tea chests can be obtained, often free of charge, from removal contractors. 'Newly second-hand' tea chests, those which have hitherto contained only tea, can be purchased for a modest sum, and are usually in better condition than those which have seen service in a dozen or so house or office removals.

Attics, junk and fringe-antique shops will sometimes yield very sound wooden boxes, dating from pre- and early post-war years: egg crates,

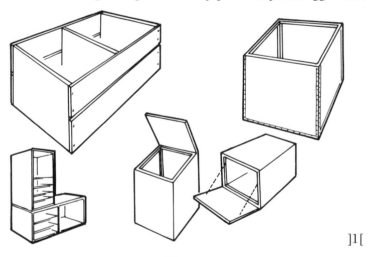

]1[

10

brewers' crates and soap boxes—the sort, in fact, which 'soap-box orators' used. Forerunners of today's corrugated cartons, these stout wooden boxes were the only means available for the bulk distribution of soap, cleaning materials, bottled products and other mass-produced articles. They were usually branded or embossed, sometimes in lurid colours, with names and advertising slogans. This 'decoration' can be removed, but cleaned up and varnished it makes a pleasant parallel with the pre-war 'street jewellery' which is now so popular.

Timber largely gave way to card, then corrugated card, and more recently, to plastic and fibre containers. Part 2 shows how many of the latter can be cleaned, painted, and put to good use for home storage.

Tea chests

Preparation

Because of their availability and their storage capacity, tea chests represent one of the quickest and easiest methods of providing storage in the home. Whether they are to be stacked for storage, or provided with padded tops as storage stool-seats, initial preparation is almost always necessary. Of light plywood construction over a stripwood frame, tea chests are usually obtained with tin-plate metal reinforcement along all edges. This protects the plywood from transit damage, but unless the chest is very new, and has been carefully handled, the metal edging can be vicious, particularly to small fingers and to clothing. So, unless it is very sound, the best plan is to remove it.

Removing the metal reinforcement

Work in stages, over a length of 150 to 200 mm (6 to 8 in) at a time. Prise the metal up at one end using a stout screwdriver, and when

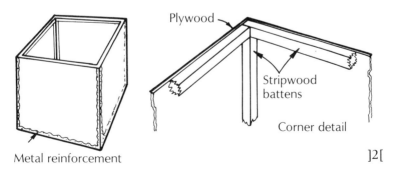

Plywood

Stripwood battens

Corner detail

Metal reinforcement

]2[

11

sufficient is free, grip the loose end firmly with pliers and pull hard. Depending on the thickness of the metal, and its condition, in doing this you'll probably pull some of the nails out. Others will remain in the wood because the metal splits or opens around the nail heads.

Hammer in new nails to replace any you have pulled out (Appendix 1). Hold a heavy object—an old kitchen scales weight, a flatiron, or even a brick will do—behind the stripwood at the spot where you're nailing to help absorb the force of the hammer blows.

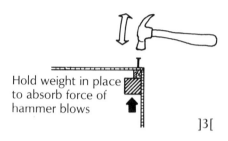

Hold weight in place
to absorb force of
hammer blows

]3[

Work your way right round the box, checking that all nails have been replaced, and that new nails are all hammered well into the wood with their heads flush with the surface.

Like so many things, this operation is much more complicated in description than in the doing. If you feel it is *too* complicated, you can decide to live with the tin strips, provided they are in good condition and haven't been worn down to razor-like edges by being dragged over concrete floors. Using the weight/flatiron/brick or whatever, work your way all round the box, until you're reasonably sure that none of the edging is going to cut flesh or fabrics.

There's no easy way to disguise these functional strips of metal, so you could turn necessity into a virtue by painting them, possibly in a bright colour to contrast with the wooden part of the box. Rub the metal down with wire wool to remove rust, and when it looks reasonably clean and bright, proceed with sanding and painting the box itself (Appendix 2).

Fitting lids or doors

If the tea chest is to be used with the open end upwards, a lid of some sort will be required. In its simplest form this could be a wooden panel with some means to stop it sliding, or it could be hinged. If the tea chest is to be placed on its side, that is with the opening at the side, a similar panel with hinging and a stay (see Appendix 7) would serve as a door.

12

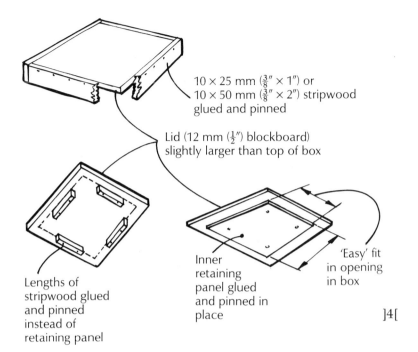

10 × 25 mm ($\frac{3}{8}'' \times 1''$) or
10 × 50 mm ($\frac{3}{8}'' \times 2''$) stripwood
glued and pinned

Lid (12 mm ($\frac{1}{2}''$) blockboard)
slightly larger than top of box

Lengths of
stripwood glued
and pinned
instead of
retaining panel

Inner
retaining
panel glued
and pinned in
place

'Easy' fit
in opening
in box

]4[

Lids

If the tea chest was supplied with a lid, this will probably be thin, damaged plywood. The only practical use for it is as a guide to the size of the box. Take it to your timber merchant and ask him to cut a piece of 12 mm ($\frac{1}{2}$ in) thick blockboard to the same size, or bigger in each direction by the amount of overhang you want.

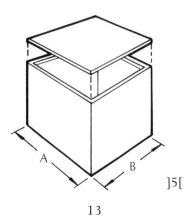

A

B

]5[

13

If the lid is missing, measure dimensions A and B, and make a note of the measurements. Don't assume that because the box *looks* square, A and B are identical. Very often they aren't. While at the timber merchant, get him to cut a piece of 12 mm ($\frac{1}{2}$ in) chipboard for the inner retaining panel if you're using this system, or to provide you with stripwood for an outer lip to stop the top sliding]4[.

Doors

Normally, the size of hinged doors will be exactly the same as the outer dimensions of the chest. Several alternative hinging arrangements are available. Appendix 7 shows hinges and related hardware such as door catches and stays, and includes information on fitting.

Altering tea chests

For reasons probably associated with the between-decks height of the holds of sailing ships, or the carrying capacity of Victorian tea-planters' labourers, tea chests, when upright, aren't desperately comfortable to sit on. They are a little too high. By reducing the height, they can make more comfortable stools, practical coffee tables, or even form the basis of a settee unit—all with inside storage space.

Tea chests are relatively easy to cut down on the long dimension. Modification along the length, however, is more difficult, and with far less effort you could produce a satisfactory purpose-made box to the exact dimensions you require.

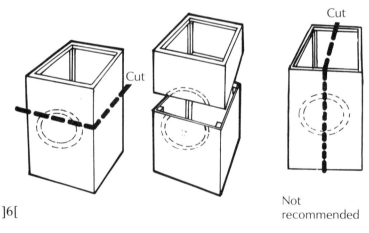

Cut

Cut

Not
recommended

]6[

14

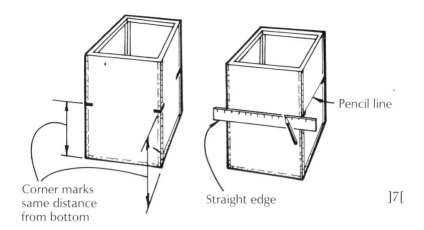

Corner marks
same distance
from bottom

Straight edge

Pencil line

]7[

First decide on the dimension you want, then measure off from the
bottom and mark the dimension at each corner. Line a straight edge up
on the marks at two of the corners, then draw a pencil line between the
marks. Repeat for the other three sides of the box, and you should have a
firm line all around the box.

Lay the box on its side and, using a small hacksaw, saw across each
corner (Appendix 1), making sure you follow the pencil line on both sides
of the corner. Continue the saw-cut only until you have cleared the
corner stripwood battens inside the box. Because it is designed to cut
metal, the hacksaw will cut through the reinforcement and any nails
which may be in its path, in addition to the wood. You can now use the
wood saw to complete the rest of the cut. You'll find that it cuts the wood
quite quickly, but would have been horribly blunted if it had been used
on metal.

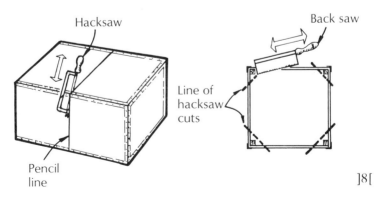

Hacksaw

Back saw

Line of
hacksaw
cuts

Pencil
line

]8[

15

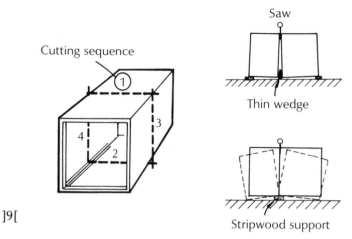

Cutting sequence

Saw

Thin wedge

Stripwood support

]9[

Turn the chest right over and cut through the side opposite the first. Then cut across the third side. By now the chest will have become distinctly wobbly, so when cutting the fourth side slide a thin wedge into the opposite slot, or provide a thin support as shown in]9[in order to stop the box trapping the saw. Cut carefully along the last 100 mm (4 in) or so, and you should have two boxes with straight, but perhaps slightly splintered, tops. Using a piece of medium sandpaper wrapped around a wooden or cork block (Appendix 1), smooth the cut edges, removing any splinters.

Replacing reinforcing battens

It is now necessary to provide stripwood battening as reinforcement, in effect duplicating that which was at the top (and bottom) of the original box. Using stripwood similar in size to the original material, mark off and cut the required lengths. Ideally they should fit firmly between the remaining corner battens.

With the box on its side, and starting with the uppermost edge, glue one side and the two ends of the first piece of new stripwood (Appendix 5). Clamp it in place, ensuring that it lines up neatly with the plywood. Using 10 mm ($\frac{3}{8}$ in) veneer or panel pins, and supporting the stripwood with the weight/flatiron/brick device mentioned earlier, hammer in two or three pins. Remove the clamps and pin evenly along the strip, at about 50 mm (2 in) centres.

Repeat until all four edges have been reinforced. Trim to a smooth, tidy finish using a block plane (Appendix 1) and then a sandpaper block. The cut-down or foreshortened tea chest can now have a lid or door fitted.

16

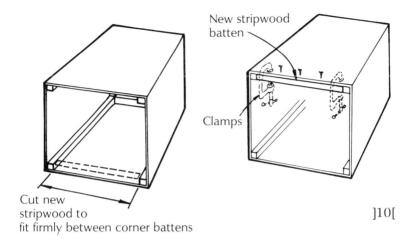

New stripwood batten

Clamps

Cut new stripwood to fit firmly between corner battens

]10[

The surplus piece of tea chest can be quite useful. One end, obviously, carries the original batten reinforcement, but the other end is un-reinforced. You could apply battening as just described, but if you want to provide a bottom for this piece of box, there's a practical short cut which obviates the battens. Cut, or get your timber merchant to cut, a piece of 12 mm ($\frac{1}{2}$ in) chipboard to the exact *inside* measurements of the box. Cut a notch in each corner to accommodate the existing battens]11[, then glue and nail it in place. When the glue has hardened, tidy up the edges with block plane and sandpaper.

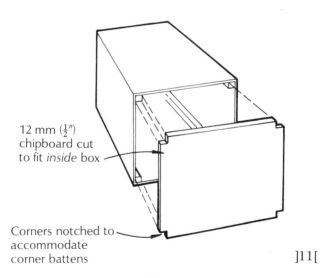

12 mm ($\frac{1}{2}''$) chipboard cut to fit *inside* box

Corners notched to accommodate corner battens

]11[

Using other ready-made wooden containers

Fruit trays, apple, orange and egg boxes, and brewer's bottle boxes are still fairly readily available and, suitably modified, can be put to very good use.

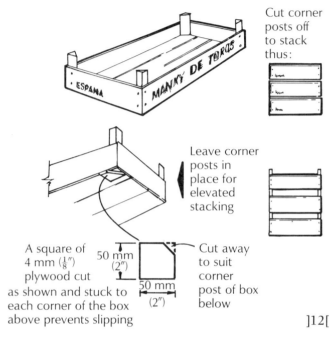

Cut corner posts off to stack thus:

Leave corner posts in place for elevated stacking

A square of 4 mm ($\frac{1}{8}''$) plywood cut as shown and stuck to each corner of the box above prevents slipping

50 mm (2'')

50 mm (2'')

Cut away to suit corner post of box below

]12[

Shallow trays provide storage for anything from correspondence to socks and handkerchiefs. Many have four triangular corner posts protruding above the box proper. These can be sawn off or, alternatively, left in place to allow you to stack them, and to see what is inside.

Apple, orange and egg boxes are generally much deeper than the trays, and often have a central divider in them. This in itself can serve as a shelf, or form a support for further shelves. Wooden containers of this type almost always have in common their method of construction: nails, and occasionally wire reinforcement.

Preparation

Remove any wire reinforcement—this usually runs around the end of the box to prevent splitting. The wire is held in place with staples, which sometimes provide the means of attaching the sides to the ends. Removing them can result in the whole tray or box falling apart! This

18

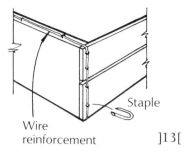

Staple

Wire
reinforcement   ]13[

isn't too big a problem if you can identify the correct positions for the various bits. If you think there is likely to be any difficulty with this operation, mark the end of each panel with a letter, and pencil the same letter on the adjacent side. The staples can generally be removed by prising them up carefully with the point of a screwdriver until sufficient is exposed to enable you to grip and pull them out with pliers.

If the box *does* fall apart, reassemble it using short nails. Before you do this, examine the inside surface of the various panels. If it is rough, and the container is to be used for something likely to be damaged by the roughness, time spent sandpapering the surfaces will be well worth while. This sandpapering is more easily done when you can lay the piece flat on a table than when the box has been reassembled.

Reassembly

The chances are, of course, that the box hasn't fallen apart, but for a better, longer-lasting job, it is as well to dismantle the box and reassemble it using glue and nails. To do this, mark your identification letters as suggested in]14[, then using a hammer and piece of waste wood, remove the side panels.

Strike block of
waste wood with hammer

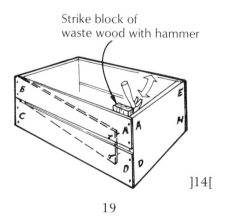

]14[

19

For safety's sake, remove the nails from each piece as it is separated. If the nails are in good condition you can keep them for reuse. Individual components can be sandpapered, but in your enthusiasm don't remove the identification letters!

Reassembly itself is quite easy. Support one of the end panels, apply glue to the edge, then reposition the side panel and drive in the requisite number of nails. Glue and nail the opposite end to the other panel, and work systematically around the whole box.

When the glue is dry, a quick rub over with the sandpaper block will remove the identity letters and any surplus glue, and the box is ready for finishing as outlined in Appendix 6.

Adapting ready-made non-wooden containers

The advent of cardboard, fibre and plastic containers marked the end of the exclusive use of timber for small packaging. It also, reasonably enough, provided the homemaker with a new range of storage opportunities. Surprisingly heavy or fragile things, such as office machines and scientific equipment, are often packed in fibre or corrugated card boxes. These containers are extraordinarily tough. Suitably decorated and with little or no reinforcement, they can be used in a variety of ways. Fibre cylindrical drums can be turned into storage stools. Rectangular containers can be painted or covered with fabric and made into occasional-use storage boxes for things such as toys, blankets and out-of-season clothing.

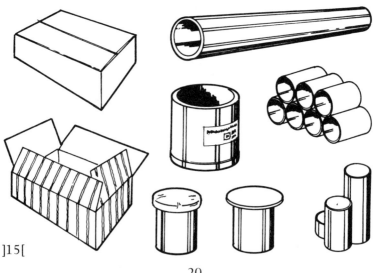

]15[

Cardboard tubes once used as 'cores' for floorcoverings, carpets and fabrics can often be cut into shorter pieces and put to good use.

Sources

Obviously, most of the containers dealt with in this section are purpose-made by or for the firms using them. Because of this you cannot normally telephone, say, a cardboard box manufacturer and ask for six boxes similar to those supplied to one of his customers. Ask for six hundred and he may be mildly interested, ask for six thousand and you'll get very good service. Ideally you need to know someone whose work allows him or her to pass on to you containers of this sort. There are, however, two types of ready-made containers which you *can* purchase: standard cardboard boxes which specialist suppliers sell to printers for packing office stationery; and fibre drums. Several manufacturers are prepared to supply containers like these in small quantities. Apart from the fact that they are relatively inexpensive, they are not contaminated by what they originally contained, which might be the case if they were obtained secondhand. And this leads to a warning: if you come across, or are offered, containers which have been used to store or transport chemicals, toxic substances or foodstuffs, give them a wide berth. All these things can, at best, make the containers smell, or prevent the paint or covering from adhering. At worst they can be *extremely dangerous.*

Manufacturers, wholesalers, retailers and stores accumulate large quantities of containers and are often only too pleased to dispose of them. An alert eye on waste skips, for instance, and a polite request, is often enough to provide the raw material for a multiplicity of storage containers.

Cardboard and fibre boxes

Converting card and fibre boxes into storage containers is easy. The extent of the work you put into them is governed, to a degree, by the time and money you wish to spend, and also by the purpose for which the container is intended. For example, a container with 'wing' top flaps can have its sides reinforced, and the hinges—the creases in the card—strengthened so that prolonged use will not cause splitting. On the other hand, a box used to store blankets, and which may be opened only two or three times a year, need not have these refinements.

Reinforcement

Where several boxes are to be stacked one on top of the other, or where weight on the top is likely to cause crushing, the sides, bottom and top

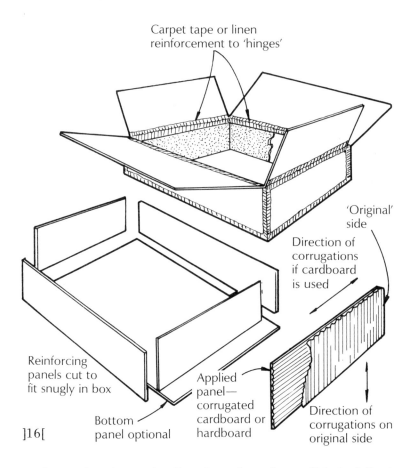

Carpet tape or linen reinforcement to 'hinges'

'Original' side

Direction of corrugations if cardboard is used

Reinforcing panels cut to fit snugly in box

Applied panel— corrugated cardboard or hardboard

Direction of corrugations on original side

Bottom panel optional

]16[

can be reinforced using hardboard panels as shown. If desired, the top flaps can be reinforced with corrugated cardboard or hardboard in a similar manner.

For a really durable job the hinging should be strengthened using linen tape similar to that used for joining the edges of carpets. This should be placed over the crease so that the tape overlaps roughly equally on either side, and then trimmed and rubbed down firmly. A slightly cheaper substitute for carpet tape is the use of dressmaker's binding tape glued in place with white PVA adhesive (Appendix 5).

Lining and covering

Boxes can be lined inside, and covered outside, with wrapping paper, wallpaper or adhesive plastic materials. If the box has been reinforced, paper is easier to use as covering or lining. Plastic materials, although in one sense more flexible, do not 'sit' and adhere so tightly to the small stepped edges which result from the application of reinforcing panels to the insides of the boxes. The manufacturer's instructions recommending allowance for shrinkage should be carefully followed when using plastics.

Wallpaper, or decorated wrapping paper, can be very attractive. Wallpaper paste is used for fixing, and once again the manufacturer's instructions should be followed.

Measuring and marking out the lining

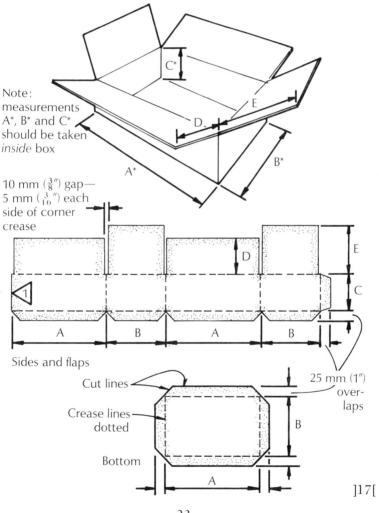

Note: measurements A*, B* and C* should be taken *inside* box

10 mm (³⁄₈") gap— 5 mm (³⁄₁₆") each side of corner crease

Sides and flaps

Cut lines

Crease lines dotted

Bottom

25 mm (1") over-laps

]17[

23

Sequence for lining

The following instructions apply to the use of paper and paste. Where adhesive plastic materials are being used, the sequence is similar, but pasting is, of course, unnecessary.

As shown in]18[, coat the bottom sheet with adhesive and place it in position, with the overlaps stuck neatly to the sides.

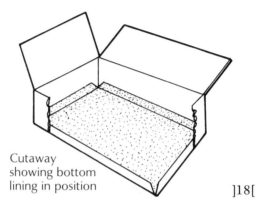

Cutaway showing bottom lining in position

]18[

Place the left-hand edge (1) into the left-hand corner of the appropriate side]19[. Position the paper so that the top overlap falls equally on to the flap. If there is no flap, fold and smooth the paper over on to the outside of the box. The lower overlap is smoothed on to the bottom of the box. Use a wallpaper paste brush or a soft, damp cloth and work the

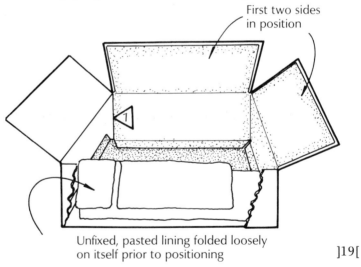

First two sides in position

Unfixed, pasted lining folded loosely on itself prior to positioning

]19[

paper tightly into the corners, easing out creases and air bubbles as you go.

Leave the box to dry off for a few hours. The paper may shrink slightly, but the overlaps will accommodate this shrinkage.

Outer covering

Cut the paper as shown in]20[. Because of the folding necessary it is not possible to provide covering for four flaps from one piece, so extra pieces will be required.

Begin by pasting and fitting the paper to the flaps, folding the overlaps around to the inside of the flaps and down on to the sides of the box.

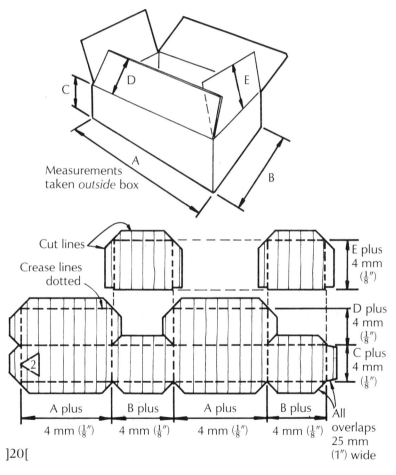

]20[

25

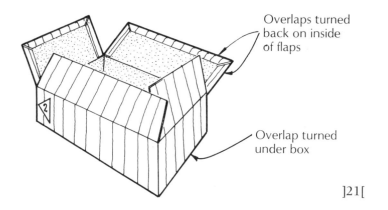

Overlaps turned
back on inside
of flaps

Overlap turned
under box

]21[

Follow with the paper for the box, dealing with the overlaps in exactly the same way.

Allow the covering to dry for at least 48 hours before putting the box into service.

Cardboard and fibre drums and cylinders

Depending on size, these can be used for all sorts of purposes ranging from storage stools for bathroom or kitchen to pigeon-hole storage for posters or drawings, and, as shown on page 69, for the tidy, orderly storage of shoes.

The drum or cylinder you have may already be the length you want. However, in all probability it won't be, so you'll have to cut it down. This is quite easy, provided that the correct marking-out sequence is followed.

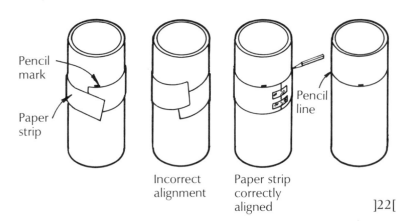

Pencil
mark

Paper
strip

Pencil
line

Incorrect
alignment

Paper strip
correctly
aligned

]22[

Marking out

For this operation you will need a soft pencil, a strip of paper with a long straight edge, and some adhesive tape. The straight edge of the paper will have to be at least three and a half times the diameter of the cylinder or drum to be cut. In other words, if the cylinder is 250 mm (10 in) across, the paper will need a straight edge at least 875 mm (35 in) long.

Mark the point on the side of the cylinder where it is to be cut. Now wrap the paper around the cylinder with the straight edge on the cutting mark. It is important to get the straight edge of the paper overlapping evenly, as shown in]22[, and it may be necessary to twist or even to re-roll the paper until it is correct.

The paper should be fairly tight on the cylinder, and when you are happy with the alignment, stick it in place with a couple of pieces of adhesive tape. Using the edge of the paper as your guide, mark a line all round the cylinder using the soft pencil.

Cutting to size

Remove the paper, and lay the cylinder on its side, providing some means to hold it firm while you work on it. The ideas in]23[may suggest other possibilities.

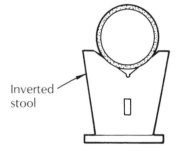

Inverted stool

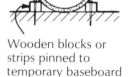

Wooden blocks or strips pinned to temporary baseboard]23[

Using your back saw, begin to cut gently into the cylinder on the 'waste' side of the pencil line. Try to hold the flat of the saw so that it is at right angles to the length of the cylinder.

When you've cut right through the wall thickness, turn the cylinder slightly away from you and continue cutting, making sure that you follow the pencil line.

As the saw-cut progresses around the cylinder, watch for the point at which the material as yet unsawn begins to collapse. Saw very gently at this stage, and if you have a helper to steady the two pieces, so much the better.

27

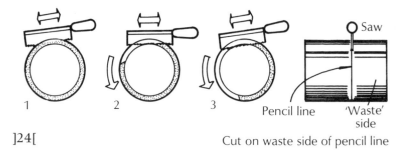

1   2   3

Saw

Pencil line   'Waste' side

]24[Cut on waste side of pencil line

When the two pieces have been separated, the sawn edges can be cleaned up with sandpaper.

Cutting cylinders at an angle

If the finished use calls for an angular cut across the cylinder, you have to follow a different procedure. The paper strip method won't work, because the strip spirals around the cylinder if you try to place it at a slope. Similarly, cutting around the cylinder progressively with a back saw is not possible. The only effective way to make an angled cut is to mark the upper limit of the slope on one side of the cylinder, and the lower limit exactly halfway round the circumference]25[. Finding the halfway mark can be done by wrapping a strip of paper around the cylinder,

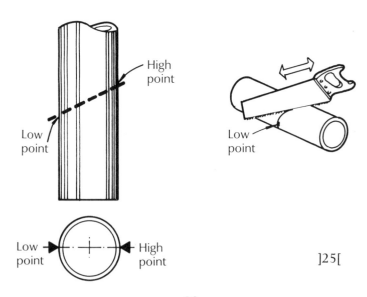

High point

Low point

Low point

Low point   High point

]25[

28

marking it so that when unrolled it shows the true circumference, and then dividing this measurement by two. The halved measurement, when transferred from the paper back on to the cylinder, will show the halfway mark. Making the cut itself will need a saw without a back, ideally a fine hand saw, because the cut must be made right through the cylinder, 'aiming' the direction of the cut so that it passes through the upper and lower limits already marked.

Fitting tops and/or bases

In their simplest form, tops and bases consist of pieces of wood, blockboard or chipboard of suitable shape, and some means of preventing them from slipping. Tops, of course, are generally removable, while bases are of similar construction, but usually fixed in place with glue and nails.]28[illustrates alternative tops and bases.

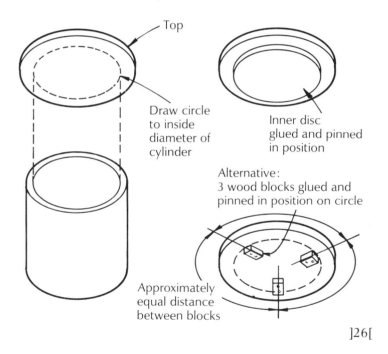

Top

Draw circle to inside diameter of cylinder

Inner disc glued and pinned in position

Alternative: 3 wood blocks glued and pinned in position on circle

Approximately equal distance between blocks

]26[

29

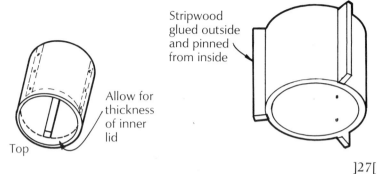

Stripwood
glued outside
and pinned
from inside

Allow for
thickness
of inner
lid

Top

]27[

Reinforcement

If the drum will have to support an appreciable weight, and depending
on the thickness of the walls, you may need to add reinforcement. This is
easily done by pinning and gluing three or more pieces of stripwood
inside (or outside) the tube.

Tops need not be circular

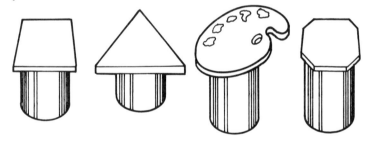

Alternative bases

Base disc glued and pinned	Larger disc base for greater stability	Fitted with skids or dome protectors	Fitted with 3 or 4 swivel castors

]28[

Further ideas for ready-made storage containers

Many of these suggestions can be developed by combining them with the ideas on pages 44 and 69.

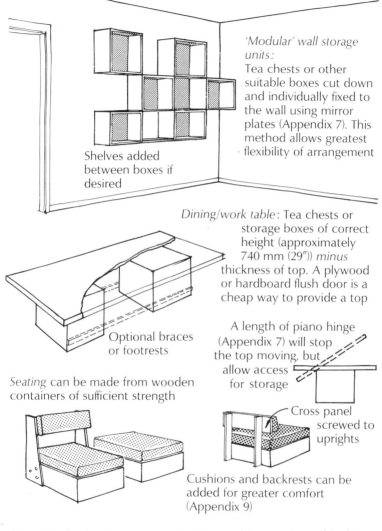

'Modular' wall storage units:
Tea chests or other suitable boxes cut down and individually fixed to the wall using mirror plates (Appendix 7). This method allows greatest flexibility of arrangement

Shelves added between boxes if desired

Dining/work table: Tea chests or storage boxes of correct height (approximately 740 mm (29")) *minus* thickness of top. A plywood or hardboard flush door is a cheap way to provide a top

A length of piano hinge (Appendix 7) will stop the top moving, but allow access for storage

Optional braces or footrests

Seating can be made from wooden containers of sufficient strength

Cross panel screwed to uprights

Cushions and backrests can be added for greater comfort (Appendix 9)

Alternative backrest arrangements: Foam rubber or plastic 'block' upholstered and fixed to wooden cross panel with 'Velcro' strip or press-studs

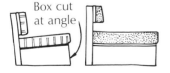

Box cut at angle

Hinged sub-seat allows access for storage

Part 2

Purpose-made storage containers

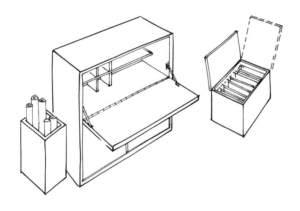

Part 2
Purpose-made storage containers

Making a storage container 'from scratch' is, naturally, a little more difficult than modifying or adapting something that already exists. Certainly more skill will be called for, but there is also more satisfaction in the use of the finished product. However, the big advantage is that the box, cabinet, or whatever will be the size and shape *you* want it to be.

Having identified the need for the container, the first stage is to *design* it. This may sound rather formal, but it is an essential step, if only to allow you to cut, or to buy, your timber economically. The first stage in design is deciding on the shape and size of the container, and how it is to open. Often, as in the case of a box which is to be placed adjacent to some other piece of furniture, length or width and height can be determined. As an example, we will take a box which is to be placed at the foot of a single bed. It could be as long as the bed is wide, should ideally be the same height as the made-up bed, and 450 to 600 mm (18 to 24 in) across.

If the container has to fit in between two fixed surfaces, be sure to make sufficient allowance for skirting-boards and any irregularities in the walls, and leave space for manoeuvring it into position.

Making a hinged-lid box in coated chipboard

Begin by drawing a simple sketch on which you mark the outside or overall dimensions. If you haven't much confidence in your drawing ability, trace sketch]30[and use it as a starting point.

Before working out the timber sizes, you will need to decide on the materials to be used. Appendix 3 will help in this decision. As explained, coated chipboard is almost universally 16 mm ($\frac{5}{8}$ in) thick, and panels are available in a range of widths from 150 to 600 mm (6 to 24 in) in steps of 75 mm (3 in).

Initial design sketch (results in waste)

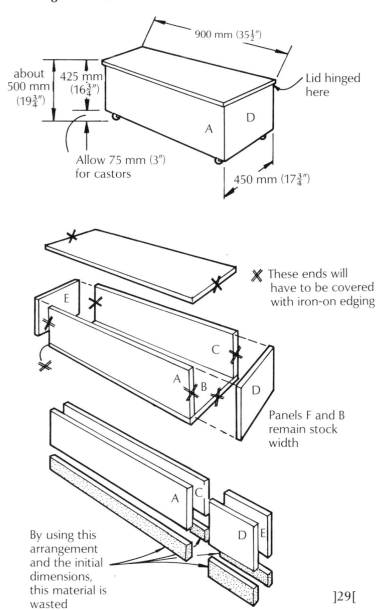

900 mm (35½")

about 500 mm (19¾")

425 mm (16¾")

Lid hinged here

A   D

Allow 75 mm (3") for castors

450 mm (17¾")

✖ These ends will have to be covered with iron-on edging

E

C

A   B   D

Panels F and B remain stock width

A   C

D   E

By using this arrangement and the initial dimensions, this material is wasted

]29[

35

Referring back to sketch]29[: how is it best to join the component parts so that the greatest use is made of standard panel widths and at the same time the number of 'raw' edges is reduced?

The box could be made as shown in]29[: it would work, and disregarding panel F for the moment, the six raw edges of panels A, B and C would have to be covered. By revising the assembly slightly, and using the full width of standard panels, as in]30[, the raw edges are reduced by

Revised design reducing waste and 'raw' edges

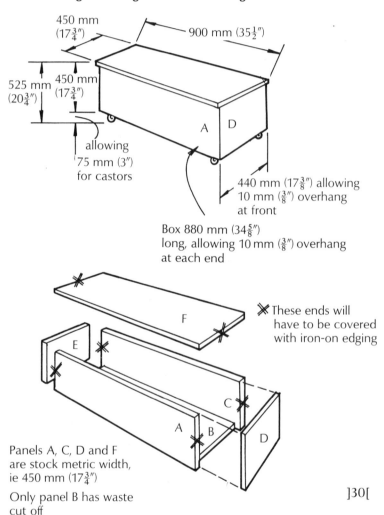

450 mm (17$\frac{3}{4}$″)

900 mm (35$\frac{1}{2}$″)

525 mm (20$\frac{3}{4}$″)

450 mm (17$\frac{3}{4}$″)

allowing 75 mm (3″) for castors

A D

440 mm (17$\frac{3}{8}$″) allowing 10 mm ($\frac{3}{8}$″) overhang at front

Box 880 mm (34$\frac{5}{8}$″) long, allowing 10 mm ($\frac{3}{8}$″) overhang at each end

F

E

C

A B

D

✳ These ends will have to be covered with iron-on edging

Panels A, C, D and F are stock metric width, ie 450 mm (17$\frac{3}{4}$″)

Only panel B has waste cut off

]30[

36

two. Also, by increasing the design height by 25 mm (1 in) or reducing the castor/foot allowance by the same amount, panels A and C need not be cut along their length.

At this point it is worth considering the available lengths of panels. Clearly, there will be less wastage, and therefore greater economy, if the component parts of the container can be provided by cutting, say, one standard 1830 mm (72 in) panel in half. This measurement is very close to that which was first decided on, and the longest panel is the top one, F. Panel F overhangs the ends slightly, so we know that the other panels will be shorter, and can therefore be cut from the standard panel.

Developing our original sketch slightly, we will imagine that we are looking straight on to the front of the box. Above, to the right of, and below, add sketches showing, respectively, the top, end view, and details of the side and bottom panels.

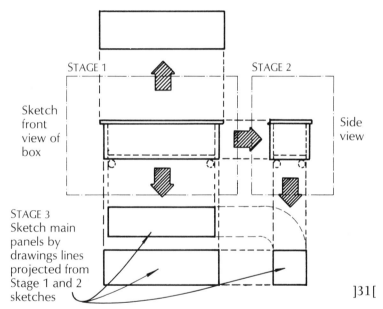

STAGE 1

STAGE 2

Sketch front view of box

Side view

STAGE 3
Sketch main panels by drawings lines projected from Stage 1 and 2 sketches

]31[

Allowing for panel thickness and overhang, the sizes of individual panels can be marked out. These are noted on the various views, resulting in a drawing which has sufficient information to prepare a cutting list for the timber merchant]32[.

This type of drawing is, in effect, a simple counterpart to an architect's 'plan and elevation'. Useful, as in this case, for the calculation of measurements, it also helps the designer visualise shape and proportion.

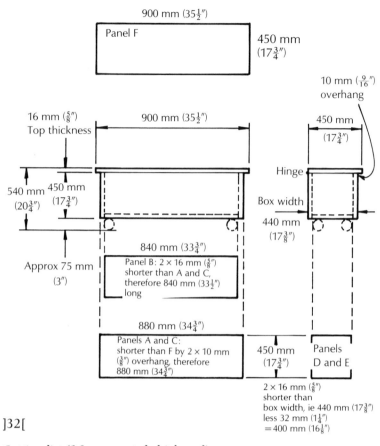

]32[

Cutting list (16 mm coated chipboard):

Panels A, C	2 required	450×880 mm	$(17\frac{3}{4} \times 34\frac{3}{4}$ in)
Panel B	1 required	400×840 mm	$(16\frac{1}{8} \times 33\frac{1}{2}$ in)
Panels D, E	2 required	400×450 mm	$(16\frac{1}{8} \times 17\frac{3}{4}$ in)
Panel F	1 required	450×900 mm	$(17\frac{3}{4} \times 35\frac{1}{2}$ in)

You will also need:

Corner connector blocks with screws 12 required
(External appearance varies according to manufacturer but principles of fitting are similar for most makes]33[)
Piano hinge (Appendix 7) with screws 1 required 880 mm ($34\frac{3}{4}$ in) length
Castors   4 required
Iron-on edging strip   3 metres (120 in)

38

Assembly

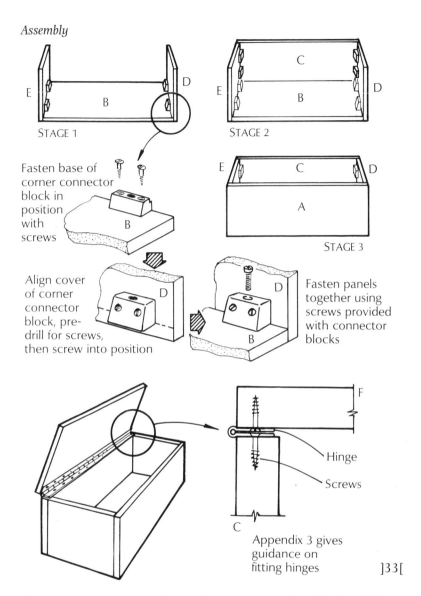

STAGE 1

STAGE 2

Fasten base of corner connector block in position with screws

STAGE 3

Align cover of corner connector block, pre-drill for screws, then screw into position

Fasten panels together using screws provided with connector blocks

Hinge

Screws

Appendix 3 gives guidance on fitting hinges

]33[

The assembly sequence is shown above. Once you have fitted the lid and castors, the remaining task is to fit the iron-on edging strip (Appendix 3). With the hinge system provided, it is as well to remember that the lid can open fully backwards, and indeed drop against the back panel, trapping unwary fingers. A lid stay (Appendix 7) might be advisable.

Making a hinged-lid box in plywood

To demonstrate how materials affect the design, cost and ease of assembly of any piece of storage furniture, we are now going to look at an alternative version of the bedding-box example. The sizes are the same, but the material is 10 mm ($\frac{3}{8}$ in) plywood. Because of the nature of plywood, corner connector blocks are replaced by glue and nails, hinges by a simple bar and bracket system, and the castors by a pair of runners. Although these modifications may represent savings in terms of cost, they will add to the time spent sandpapering, then painting or varnishing.

The design/cutting list on page 38 can be repeated almost exactly for this version of the box. But we are less concerned with the need to use standard or stock panel measurements because the plywood will probably be cut from large sheets (Appendix 3).

Initial design sketches

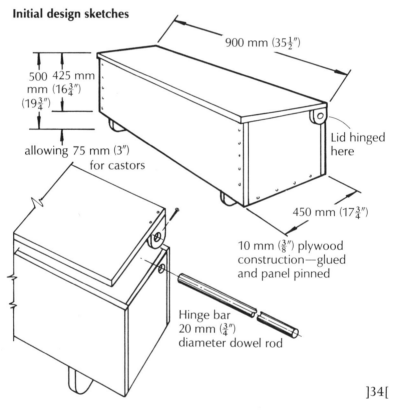

900 mm ($35\frac{1}{2}$")

500 mm ($19\frac{3}{4}$") 425 mm ($16\frac{3}{4}$")

allowing 75 mm (3") for castors

Lid hinged here

450 mm ($17\frac{3}{4}$")

10 mm ($\frac{3}{8}$") plywood construction—glued and panel pinned

Hinge bar 20 mm ($\frac{3}{4}$") diameter dowel rod

]34[

In this design, the bar and bracket hinge system will consist of two shaped plywood blocks attached to the lid. The blocks are drilled to take a 16 mm ($\frac{5}{8}$ in) diameter dowel rod (dowelling is wood, usually hardwood, machined into the shape of a round rod or bar) which passes through similar holes drilled in the ends of the box]34[. This system restricts the opening of the lid to a point a little beyond the vertical position.

Working out the panel sizes for the plywood box is done in the same way as for the previous version, bearing in mind that the material thickness this time is 10 mm ($\frac{3}{8}$ in).

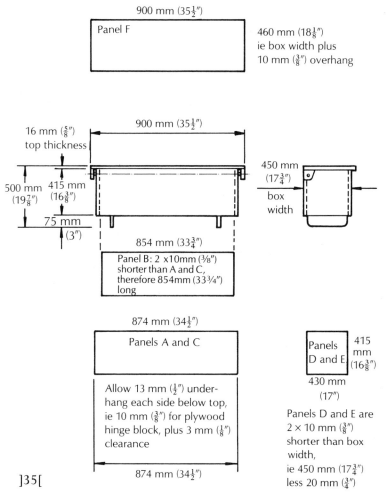

900 mm (35$\frac{1}{2}$")

Panel F

460 mm (18$\frac{1}{8}$")
ie box width plus
10 mm ($\frac{3}{8}$") overhang

16 mm ($\frac{5}{8}$")
top thickness

900 mm (35$\frac{1}{2}$")

500 mm (19$\frac{7}{8}$")   415 mm (16$\frac{3}{8}$")

75 mm ($3''$)

854 mm (33$\frac{3}{4}$")

Panel B: 2 x10mm (³/₈")
shorter than A and C,
therefore 854mm (33¾")
long

450 mm (17$\frac{3}{4}$")
box width

874 mm (34$\frac{1}{2}$")

Panels A and C

Allow 13 mm ($\frac{1}{2}$") under-
hang each side below top,
ie 10 mm ($\frac{3}{8}$") for plywood
hinge block, plus 3 mm ($\frac{1}{8}$")
clearance

874 mm (34$\frac{1}{2}$")

Panels D and E   415 mm (16$\frac{3}{8}$")

430 mm (17")

Panels D and E are
2 × 10 mm ($\frac{3}{8}$")
shorter than box
width,
ie 450 mm (17$\frac{3}{4}$")
less 20 mm ($\frac{3}{4}$")

]35[

41

Cutting list (10 mm plywood):

Panels A, C	2 required	874×415 mm	$(34\frac{1}{2} \times 16\frac{3}{8}$ in)
Panel B	1 required	854×430 mm	$(33\frac{3}{4} \times 17$ in)
Panels D, E	2 required	430×415 mm	$(16\frac{3}{8} \times 17$ in)
Panel F	1 required	900×460 mm	$(35\frac{1}{2} \times 18\frac{1}{8}$ in)

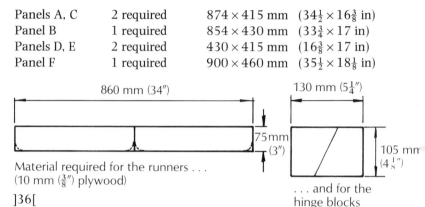

860 mm (34″)

130 mm ($5\frac{1}{4}$″)

75mm (3″)

105 mm ($4\frac{1}{8}$″)

Material required for the runners ...
(10 mm ($\frac{3}{8}$″) plywood)

]36[

... and for the hinge blocks

You will also need a piece of 20 mm ($\frac{3}{4}$ in) diameter dowelling for the hinge bar, 50 mm (2 in) longer than panel F to allow for trimming.

Assembly

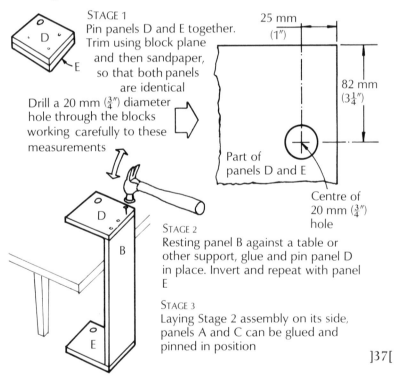

STAGE 1
Pin panels D and E together. Trim using block plane and then sandpaper, so that both panels are identical

Drill a 20 mm ($\frac{3}{4}$″) diameter hole through the blocks working carefully to these measurements

25 mm (1″)

82 mm ($3\frac{1}{4}$″)

Part of panels D and E

Centre of 20 mm ($\frac{3}{4}$″) hole

STAGE 2
Resting panel B against a table or other support, glue and pin panel D in place. Invert and repeat with panel E

STAGE 3
Laying Stage 2 assembly on its side, panels A and C can be glued and pinned in position

]37[

42

Assembly

The assembly sequence is shown in]37[. Make the hinge blocks as shown in]38[and glue and pin the separated blocks to the edges of the lid, ensuring that they are the same distance from the back of the panel.

Place the lid in position on the box, then pass the dowel rod right through all four holes and hammer a panel pin through each block into the rod. Using the back saw trim off the surplus rod.

The runners]36[can now be made and fitted at an equal distance in from each end of the box. Use glue, and panel pins driven into the tops of the runners from inside the box.

Finished and painting (Appendix 6) complete the plywood version.

The foregoing techniques will almost certainly apply to the construction of virtually any purpose-made storage container, whether it be a small box, or the carcass of a wardrobe.

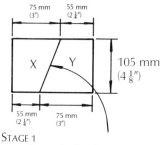

STAGE 1
Saw through this line, turn one piece around and stack it on the other

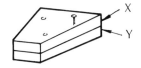

STAGE 2
Pin the blocks together, trim with block plane and then sandpaper. Round the lower edges off thus:

STAGE 3
Drill a 20 mm (3¼") diameter hole through both blocks

STAGE 4
Separate the blocks

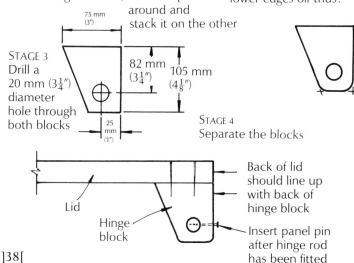

Lid

Hinge block

Back of lid should line up with back of hinge block

Insert panel pin after hinge rod has been fitted

]38[

43

Further ideas for purpose-made storage containers
Many of these suggestions can be developed by combining them
with the ideas on pages 31 and 69.

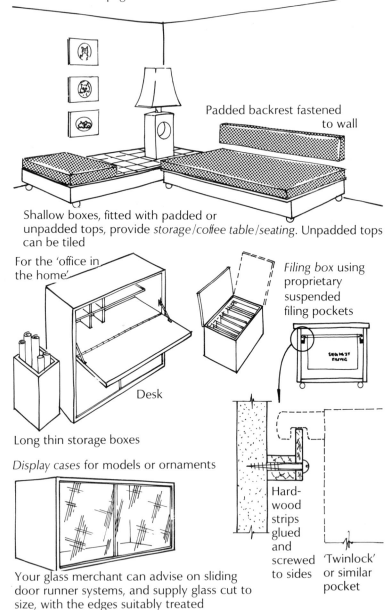

Padded backrest fastened
to wall

Shallow boxes, fitted with padded or
unpadded tops, provide *storage/coffee table/seating.* Unpadded tops
can be tiled

For the 'office in
the home'

Filing box using
proprietary
suspended
filing pockets

Desk

Long thin storage boxes

Display cases for models or ornaments

Hard-
wood
strips
glued
and
screwed
to sides

'Twinlock'
or similar
pocket

Your glass merchant can advise on sliding
door runner systems, and supply glass cut to
size, with the edges suitably treated

Part 3

Shelving

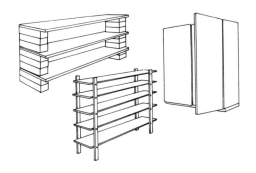

Part 3
Shelving

Shelves are a basic part of any storage system, and can be made quite easily.

There are three alternatives open to us: the use of existing side-supports for shelves, such as the alcove at the side of a fireplace; the use of brackets fixed to a wall or other surface; or the provision of free-standing shelving.

Using existing side-supports

There isn't a great deal to the design of shelving to fit between the walls of an alcove or recess. Clearly one needs to know the distance between the shelves, from which one can decide on the number. For reasons which will soon become obvious, it is best to have the shelves cut 25 to 50 mm (1 to 2 in) longer than the space available for them.

Although one or two proprietary systems have been designed which wedge a shelf between the walls of the recess, we'll concentrate on the simpler, cheaper and more reliable system of fixing battens on the side walls, and laying the shelves between them.

In old properties, it is as well to consider potential hazards such as concealed water and gas pipes and, somewhat less likely, hidden electricity cables, before deciding which alcove or recess to use. Alcoves were the natural result of building out a chimney breast, and curious back-boiler and other plumbing systems were often embodied, particularly in lower floors. Similarly, gas pipes sometimes fed stoves and gas lighting brackets. Conversion or decoration at some time in the past may have concealed these, and while you could reasonably expect such pipes *not* to contain water or gas, they may do! Water pipes, particularly, were sometimes used as part of a system in a neighbouring terraced house. Gas pipes might have been capped off and remained unused since some previous occupant's Victorian aunt complained of the effect of gaslight on her complexion, but one end *could* still be connected to a gas supply.

You're going to be drilling holes to take your shelf battens. Holes in water pipes can be messy, embarrassing if they're your neighbour's water pipes, and expensive to repair. Holes in gas pipes or electricity cables are downright dangerous!

The following hints may help in detecting these hidden hazards: look for any suspicious bulges in the plaster, or pipes which come out of (or disappear into) the wall you're concerned with. It's sometimes possible in this way to trace the route of pipes, but if in doubt, find another alcove. If funds permit, you can resort to the more scientific method of hiring a gadget to help you trace pipes and cables. Like a miniature mine-detector, when run over the wall it bleeps or flashes a light when it senses pipes within a few millimetres of the surface. Not infallible, but fun.

Another thing to watch for is walls which bulge, are hollow, or are not vertical. Stud and plaster walls – which generally consist of timber uprights ('studs') sandwiched between layers of lath and plaster, or plaster board – may not take the weight of the shelving unless the screws for the shelf brackets are driven through the plaster and into the studs. Walls

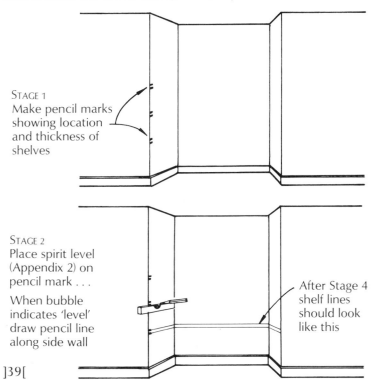

STAGE 1
Make pencil marks showing location and thickness of shelves

STAGE 2
Place spirit level (Appendix 2) on pencil mark . . .

When bubble indicates 'level' draw pencil line along side wall

After Stage 4 shelf lines should look like this

]39[

which bulge or are not vertical may look peculiar as the shelves will not all be the same length. The installation sequence shown in]39/40[will help ensure that you compensate for curved or out-of-true walls.

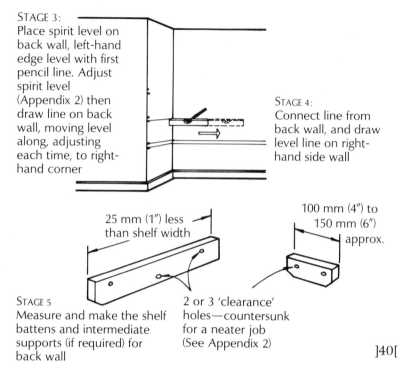

STAGE 3:
Place spirit level on back wall, left-hand edge level with first pencil line. Adjust spirit level (Appendix 2) then draw line on back wall, moving level along, adjusting each time, to right-hand corner

STAGE 4:
Connect line from back wall, and draw level line on right-hand side wall

25 mm (1") less than shelf width

100 mm (4") to 150 mm (6") approx.

STAGE 5
Measure and make the shelf battens and intermediate supports (if required) for back wall

2 or 3 'clearance' holes—countersunk for a neater job (See Appendix 2)

]40[

Place the appropriate batten against the pencil line representing the underside of the shelf. Use a sharp nail or bradawl (Appendix 1) to mark the position of the screw holes on the wall. Remove the batten, then drill and plug the holes in the wall, as shown in Appendix 9.

Screw the battens in place. When they are all securely fixed, measure and note the length of each shelf. This step has been left to the last to ensure that, even if the walls bulge or are not vertical, the shelves will be level, although they may not all be the same length.

The shelves should be 3 to 5 mm ($\frac{1}{8}$ to $\frac{3}{16}$ in) shorter than the 'tight' length (that is, the exact distance between the walls). When placed in position they should fit without 'jamming' against the walls. In extreme cases it may be necessary to plane or sandpaper them down.

The shelves can be left resting unfixed on the battens, which makes for easy removal for cleaning or decorating. However, for greater security a

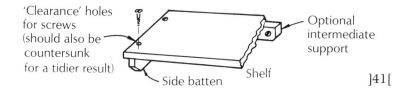

'Clearance' holes for screws (should also be countersunk for a tidier result) — Side batten — Shelf — Optional intermediate support

]41[

couple of screws can be driven through each end of the shelves into the battens.

Fixing shelving against walls

If the walls are sound enough, and the room layout warrants, shelves can be fixed to the walls by one of several methods.

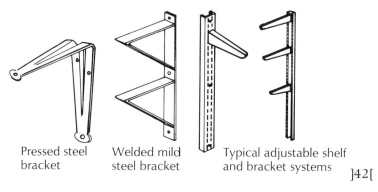

Pressed steel bracket

Welded mild steel bracket

Typical adjustable shelf and bracket systems

]42[

Pressed steel brackets are cheapest and simplest, and the preliminary steps are similar for most systems, so, for our example, we will assume that brackets of this type are being used.

If the wall is of the stud and plaster type, it is almost always essential to position the brackets or uprights against each stud. It is not always easy to locate the studs. Sometimes there is visible indication – a bulge or slight bowing in the wall, or a line of nail or screw holes. Try tapping the wall at intervals. If the hollow sound changes, and becomes less hollow, that is because you are tapping over or near a stud.

Deciding on the number and position of the brackets on a solid brick or stone wall can be done using pencil and paper, as a design exercise, but as you will have to mark the wall out anyway, you could go straight to this stage.

Decide on the length of the shelves, their distance from the floor, and the space between them. Using the spirit level, draw the edge of each shelf in

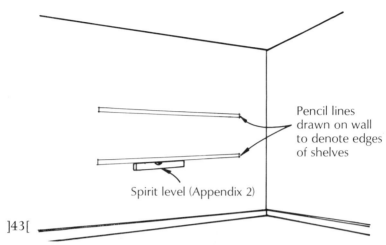

Pencil lines drawn on wall to denote edges of shelves

Spirit level (Appendix 2)

]43[

its position on the wall]43[. If, for instance, the shelves are 20 mm ($\frac{13}{16}$ in) thick, you should end up with two lines 20 mm ($\frac{13}{16}$ in) apart, over the length of the shelving, the top line denoting the top of the shelf and the bottom line the underside.

The distance between the brackets will depend to some extent on the weight the shelves will have to support. There are no hard and fast rules for this, but a good starting point is to divide the shelf length into quarters, and place a bracket one quarter in from each end. For longer shelves, one or more intermediate brackets will be required. Try to ensure that not more than 450 mm (18 in) of shelf is unsupported, or 300 mm (12 in) if the items to be stored on the shelf are very heavy.

To find the distance between centres of brackets]44[

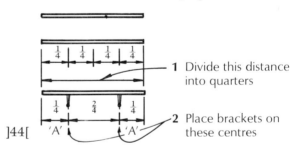

1 Divide this distance into quarters

2 Place brackets on these centres

]44['A' 'A'

Dimension 'A' should not exceed 450 mm (18")—or 300 mm (12") for heavy loads; if it does, work to diagram]45a[opposite:

Where intermediate brackets are required to support long runs of shelving, their position can be determined as shown in]45b[and]45c[.

50

Long shelves

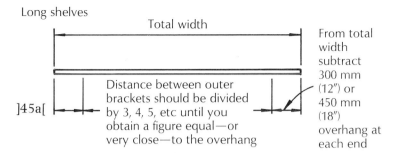

Total width

From total width subtract 300 mm (12″) or 450 mm (18″) overhang at each end

Distance between outer brackets should be divided by 3, 4, 5, etc until you obtain a figure equal—or very close—to the overhang

]45a[

Example (metric)

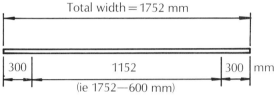

Total width = 1752 mm

300 | 1152 | 300 | mm

(ie 1752—600 mm)

1152 divided by 3 = 384 mm (Answer A)
1152 mm divided by 4 = 288 mm (Answer B)

Answer B is closer to 300 mm than Answer A, therefore bracket centres can be marked out as follows, and five brackets will be needed for each shelf:

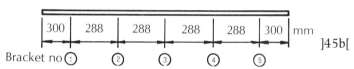

300 | 288 | 288 | 288 | 288 | 300 | mm

]45b[

Bracket no ① ② ③ ④ ⑤

Example (imperial)

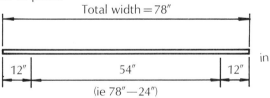

Total width = 78″

12″ | 54″ | 12″ | in

(ie 78″—24″)

54″ divided by 3 = 18″ (Answer A)
54″ divided by 4 = 13½″ (Answer B)

Answer B is closer to 12″ than Answer A, therefore bracket centres can be marked out as follows:

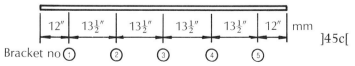

12″ | 13½″ | 13½″ | 13½″ | 13½″ | 12″ | mm

]45c[

Bracket no ① ② ③ ④ ⑤

Returning to our example]45a, b and c[: five brackets will be needed for each shelf. On the lowest pencil line on the wall we mark 300 mm (12 in) in from one end, then make four marks 288 mm (10 in) apart, and if our arithmetic has worked, we should have a distance of 300 mm (12 in) to the other end of the shelf.

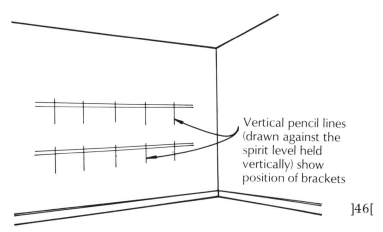

Vertical pencil lines (drawn against the spirit level held vertically) show position of brackets

]46[

Using the spirit level, but vertically this time, draw a pencil line upwards and downwards from each bracket centre line, extending to the underside of the highest shelf. If you are using pressed metal brackets, hold the bracket against the wall with the lowest screw hole on the centre line, and the upper screw holes straddling it equally. Because the metal bends away from you it isn't always easy to see that the top of the bracket is exactly level with the line denoting the underside of the shelf. A

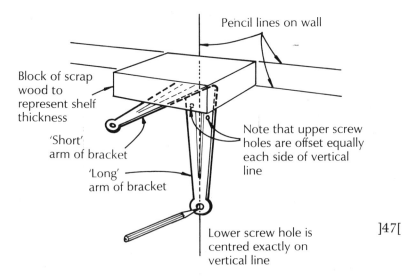

Pencil lines on wall

Block of scrap wood to represent shelf thickness

'Short' arm of bracket

'Long' arm of bracket

Note that upper screw holes are offset equally each side of vertical line

Lower screw hole is centred exactly on vertical line

]47[

small block of wood, in effect representing a small bit of the shelf, held as shown in]47[, will help.

Drill and plug the holes (Appendix 8) and screw the brackets to the wall.

The shelves may now be placed in position, and should 'sit' straight and level. They should be secured with screws passing up into the shelves through the screw holes in the bracket.

Fixing adjustable shelf systems to a wall

With adjustable shelf systems it is very important that the upright supports are really upright, not only when seen from the front, but also relative to the wall. Here again, watch out for bulging or non-vertical walls.

Typical adjustable shelf support system

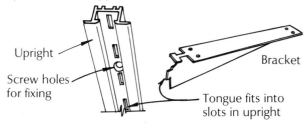

Upright

Bracket

Screw holes for fixing

Tongue fits into slots in upright

]48[

Decide on spacing of supports, following the advice on pages 50 and 51. This time, however, it isn't necessary to draw the shelves on the wall because they are adjustable anyway. The important lines are those representing the centres of the uprights, and the lines of the fixing screws. Aim to draw a diagram on the wall like that in]49[, using the spirit level.

Drill and plug the holes (Appendix 8) then, using the spirit level, check that the uprights are vertical, in case the wall isn't. It may be necessary to insert packing pieces, as shown in]50[, to compensate for bulges or curves in the wall.

Following the manufacturer's instructions, position the brackets at selected intervals. Place the shelves in position and use the spirit level to check that they are horizontal. If the preliminary steps have been followed, there should be no difficulty in this respect, but again minor adjustments can be made by using thin plywood packing pieces between the shelves and the brackets, or by adjusting the packing between the uprights and the wall. Major misalignment, however, calls for more drastic measures. Because it is almost impossible to re-drill holes very

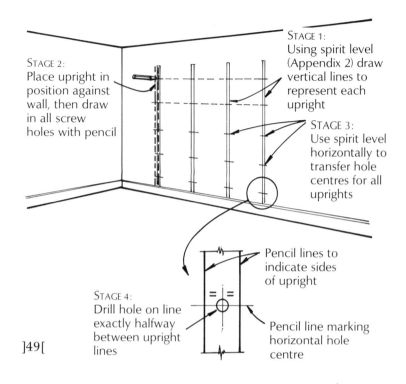

STAGE 1:
Using spirit level (Appendix 2) draw vertical lines to represent each upright

STAGE 2:
Place upright in position against wall, then draw in all screw holes with pencil

STAGE 3:
Use spirit level horizontally to transfer hole centres for all uprights

Pencil lines to indicate sides of upright

STAGE 4:
Drill hole on line exactly halfway between upright lines

Pencil line marking horizontal hole centre

]49[

Minor corrections to adjustable shelf system uprights

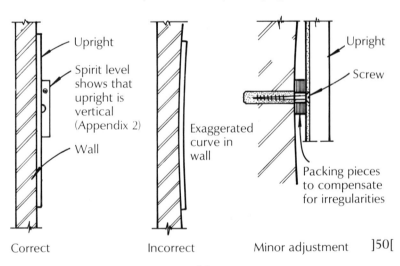

Upright

Spirit level shows that upright is vertical (Appendix 2)

Wall

Exaggerated curve in wall

Upright

Screw

Packing pieces to compensate for irregularities

Correct

Incorrect

Minor adjustment

]50[

close to existing ones, one must reposition the uprights slightly to one side or the other of the original holes, in effect starting again and working more accurately!

When you're satisfied with the levels and positions of the shelves, they can be secured to the brackets using short screws. It's worth noting that with most adjustable shelving systems, once the shelves have been fixed to the brackets, the level of the shelves can only be adjusted after the screws have been removed. A tedious job if you happen to have a dozen or so brackets with four screws in each!

Free-standing shelves

Many people associate shelving with walls and, reasonably enough, a sound wall makes a good support on which to fix shelving. However, where walls are not suitable, or where wall space is limited, free-standing shelves can be used against the wall, or to divide one part of a room from another. While free-standing shelves are normally quite steady, if they are heavily laden or over 1500 mm (60 in) high it is a good idea to secure one end, at least, to a wall.

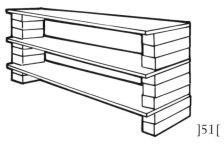

]51[

The simplest shelves in this category are made by laying planks between stacks of bricks, as shown above. Up to a height of about 11 bricks, shelves built in this way can be quite stable, but above that height beware of the very real danger of collapse, particularly where small children are likely to pull on them for support.

Designing shelves

Shelves, and their natural counterpart, cupboards (see page 61), are subject to the same preliminary design stages as the hinged-lid box described in Part 2.

You will need to measure the available space and decide upon the limiting length, height and width (the front to back measurement) of the finished shelving.

First design sketch

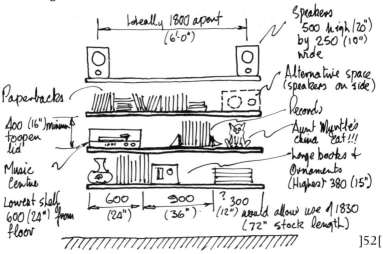

Ideally 1800 apart
(6'-0")

Speakers
500 high (20")
by 250 (10")
wide

Alternative space
(speakers on side)

Paperbacks

Records

400 (16") minimum
to open
lid

Aunt Myrtle's
china cat !!!

Music
Centre

Large books +
Ornaments
(Highest 380 (15")

Lowest shelf
600 (24") from
floor

600   900   ? 300
(24")   (36")   (12") would allow use of 1830
                       (72" stock length)

]52[

A design sketch will help you decide on the number of shelves and the distance between them. Shelves for paperback and other books need not be more than 230 to 250 mm (9 to 10 in) apart. Large books, on the other hand, can occupy a height of 380 mm (15 in) or more if they are to stand upright. If the shelves are to carry things other than books, a few minutes' thought, and a few quick measurements, will give us enough information for our first design sketch, which may look something like]52[.

**First design sketch used to work out
measurement and cutting/material list**

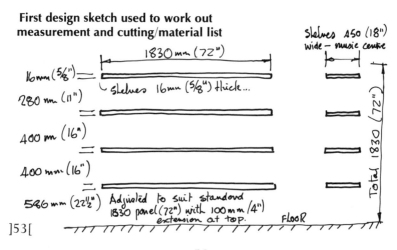

Shelves 450 (18")
wide — music centre

1830 mm (72")

16mm (5/8")

Shelves 16mm (5/8") thick...

280 mm (11")

400 mm (16")

400 mm (16")

Total 1830 (72")

586 mm (22½") Adjusted to suit standard
1830 panel (72") with 100 mm (4")
extension at top.

FLOOR

]53[

56

Begin by drawing the shelves, omitting the sides at this stage. On the shelves draw simple boxes or shapes to represent the items they are to carry.

Mark the various sizes, then add them up to arrive at an approximate (or desired) length. This can now be related to the space available, or the extent to which you want the shelves to divide the room. Then, as with the hinged-lid box in Part 2, the final measurements are related to available material.

The options: solid or open-sided shelves

So far, the shelves in the design are unsupported. We have at least two options here. We can decide on solid-sided shelves, in which the support for the shelves is provided by two or more upright panels, ideally of the same width and material as the shelves themselves. Alternatively, we can opt for 'ladder'-sided shelves, with two or more ladder-like supports.

Returning to design sketch]52[: if solid sides are to be used, we must decide whether the sides are to stop level with the top shelf, or whether they are to extend above the top shelf to provide support for books.

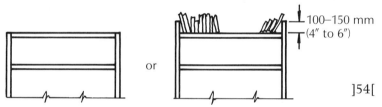

The final design sketch shows the measurements of the panels needed, and enables us to prepare a cutting list:

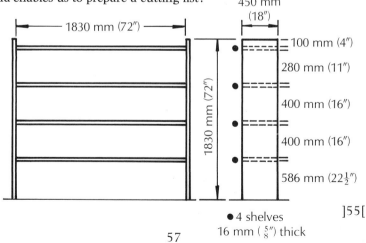

]55[

• 4 shelves
16 mm ($\frac{5}{8}''$) thick

Cutting list:

| Shelves | 4 required | 1830 × 450 mm | (72 × 17¾ in) |
| Sides | 2 required | 1830 × 450 mm | (72 × 17¾ in) |

The construction of sides for ladder-sided shelves is dealt with on pages 63–66.

Constructing solid-sided shelves

The most important part of constructing this type of shelving is getting the sides, and the vertical distance between each shelf, identical. For this example we'll assume that we are using coated chipboard and corner connector blocks (page 39).

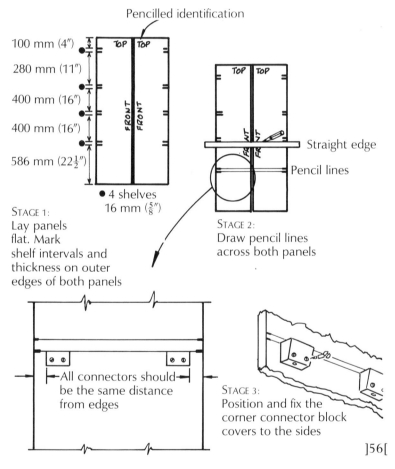

Pencilled identification

100 mm (4″)
280 mm (11″)
400 mm (16″)
400 mm (16″)
586 mm (22½″)

• 4 shelves
16 mm (⅝″)

Straight edge
Pencil lines

STAGE 1:
Lay panels
flat. Mark
shelf intervals and
thickness on outer
edges of both panels

STAGE 2:
Draw pencil lines
across both panels

All connectors should
be the same distance
from edges

STAGE 3:
Position and fix the
corner connector block
covers to the sides

]56[

58

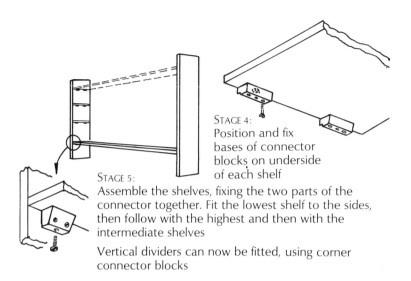

STAGE 4:
Position and fix
bases of connector
blocks on underside
of each shelf

STAGE 5:
Assemble the shelves, fixing the two parts of the
connector together. Fit the lowest shelf to the sides,
then follow with the highest and then with the
intermediate shelves

Vertical dividers can now be fitted, using corner
connector blocks

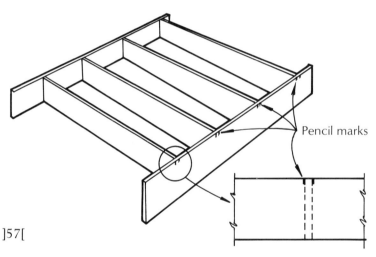

Pencil marks

]57[

Backing

The cheapest and simplest material for backing solid-sided shelves is
hardboard. However, it has the disadvantage of having one smooth, and
one rough surface. A more expensive alternative is 3 mm ($\frac{1}{8}$ in) plywood.

Measuring backing: Measure the overall width of the shelves, including
the sides, and the height. Cut, or have cut, a panel to these

measurements. If, because of the size, you cannot obtain one panel as a complete piece, arrange two panels so that the joint falls exactly midway on a shelf.

Fitting backing: If the backing is to be painted or varnished, this is best done *before* fixing—unless the shelves are to be painted as well as the backing. When coated chipboard has been used for the shelves, pre-painting of the backing saves a lot of mess and time spent wiping paint marks off the coating.

Place the shelf assembly face downwards on a firm flat surface. Assuming that the backing will be panel-pinned or screwed in place, make pencil marks on the outside of the sides to show the thickness of each shelf.

Run a line of adhesive (Appendix 5) 2 or 3 mm ($\frac{1}{16}$ or $\frac{1}{8}$ in) wide along the edges of the sides and the shelves. Lower the panel carefully into position, as accurately as possible because a lot of subsequent sliding and

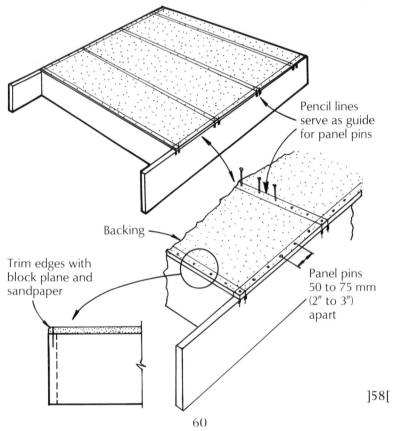

Pencil lines serve as guide for panel pins

Backing

Trim edges with block plane and sandpaper

Panel pins 50 to 75 mm (2″ to 3″) apart

]58[

adjustment can displace the adhesive. If the panel has been accurately cut, it should fit neatly over the shelves, but it can happen that in laying the shelves face downwards, the whole assembly has distorted, in which case, ease diagonally opposite corners gently so that they match exactly with the panel edges. As a final check, you could test the squareness of the sides at the top and bottom using a try square (Appendix 2).

Now extend the lines denoting the shelf centres from the sides on to the back panel, and using a straight edge draw two lines the whole width of the panel for each shelf]58[.

Working from the centre of each shelf towards the sides, hammer in panel pins at 50 to 75 mm (2 to 3 in) centres. When all the shelves have been pinned, continue pinning the panel to the edges of the sides. If you're very confident that you can judge the centre of the side pieces omit the pencil line.

When the adhesive is dry, clean up the edges of the back panel using a block plane and sandpaper, for greater tidiness providing a slight bevel at the corners.

Turning shelves into cupboards

A cupboard is no more than solid-sided shelving with doors fitted between individual shelves, or covering the entire front of the assembly. The doors can be of coated chipboard or plywood, or (funds permitting) you can fit ready-made louvred doors. Guidance on hinges and catches is given in Appendix 7.

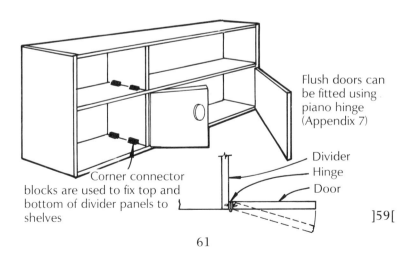

Flush doors can be fitted using piano hinge (Appendix 7)

Divider
Hinge
Door

Corner connector blocks are used to fix top and bottom of divider panels to shelves

]59[

61

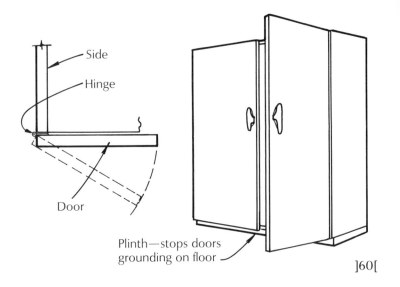

Side

Hinge

Door

Plinth—stops doors
grounding on floor

]60[

Where doors extend to the base of the cabinet, a plinth or some other support is necessary so that the doors swing clear of the floor. The following diagram shows the construction of a simple plinth:

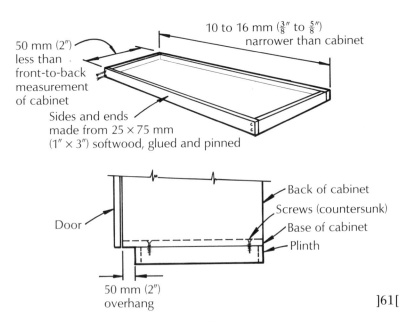

10 to 16 mm ($\frac{3}{8}''$ to $\frac{5}{8}''$) narrower than cabinet

50 mm (2″) less than front-to-back measurement of cabinet

Sides and ends made from 25 × 75 mm (1″ × 3″) softwood, glued and pinned

Door

Back of cabinet

Screws (countersunk)

Base of cabinet

Plinth

50 mm (2″) overhang

]61[

62

Ladder-sided shelves

Several proprietary ladder-sided shelving systems are available; all carry complete instructions and all tend to be quite expensive so we will concentrate on making our own 'ladders'.

As with solid-sided shelves, you need to know length, height and width. Having decided on these measurements, there are two alternatives: either to place a crossbar at each of the designed levels—which restricts you in the future to those levels; or to provide a number of equally spaced bars, so giving the option of future adjustment. These bars can be placed at 75, 100 or 150 mm (3, 4 or 6 in) intervals, and for our example we will work on the latter measurement.

It is necessary to decide on how many ladders you are going to need for the particular set of shelves. Unlike solid-sided shelves the ladders need not (indeed *should* not) be placed at the extreme ends. By placing them, say, 300 mm (12 in) in from each end, you reduce the unsupported length of shelf—in our example leaving 1230 mm (48 in) unsupported. With reasonable shelving timber this is unlikely to deflect downwards.

Design sketch

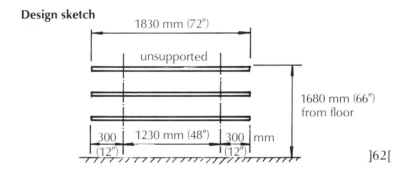

]62[

A greater interval between supports, as in]63[, would call for one or more intermediate ladders and cross-bracing, particularly if the shelves are not secured to a wall or some other structure.

Design sketch

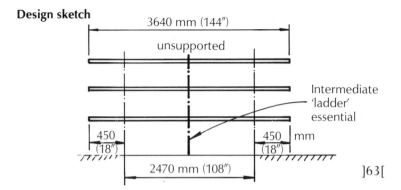

]63[

Returning to design sketch]62[: the height is 1680 mm (66 in) to the top shelf. If the ladder 'rungs' are going to be 150 mm (6 in) apart,]64[shows that 11 rungs will be needed. Extending the ladder above the top shelf will call for a final, twelfth rung.

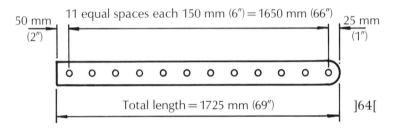

]64[

Having determined the length of the stripwood ladder sides, we will now consider the width of the ladder to arrive at the amount of dowelling you are going to need.

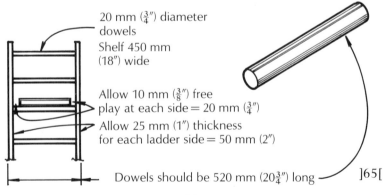

]65[

64

Making the 'ladders'

STAGE 1: Mark out the sides

Mark centre line along whole length of 25 × 50 or 75 mm (1″ × 2″ or 3″) softwood

Use try square (Appendix 2) to mark cross-lines at 150 mm (6″) intervals

STAGE 2: Stack and clamp sides

Marked-out side clamped to top of evenly stacked pile of remaining sides

'G' clamps

Workbench or tabletop protected against drill damage by piece of thin waste wood

STAGE 3: Drill holes

20 mm (¾″) diameter drill 'bit' (Appendix 1) held as near vertical as possible when drilling through all four sides

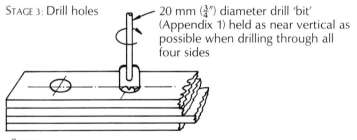

STAGE 4:
Unclamp and separate the sides. If desired radius the top edges. Use a tin or other round object to mark out the shape, and a coping saw (Appendix 1) for cutting

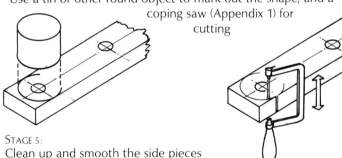

STAGE 5:
Clean up and smooth the side pieces using a block plane and sandpaper

]66[

Assembling the ladders

Check that the dowel rods are all the same length. Apply white PVA adhesive (Appendix 5) to the inside of the holes in one of the ladder sides. Ease the dowels gently into position, if necessary tapping them with a mallet until the end of each dowel is flush with the outer surface of the wood. Now glue the inside of the holes of the matching side, and feed the free ends of the dowels into the corresponding holes. They are very unlikely at first to be positioned correctly so that they all move neatly into place, and it will almost certainly be necessary to deflect some of the dowels until they line up. Gently thumping the stripwood with the mallet when alignment is almost correct will help.

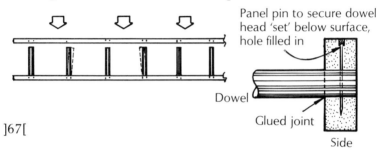

]67[

The dowels should pass through the holes of the opposite ladder side until the ends are flush with the outer surface of the wood. This is one of those woodworking exercises calling for a little patience and rather more dexterity, but you should end up with a reasonably 'square' ladder. Lay this flat on a table or the floor, and drive a 37 mm ($1\frac{1}{2}$ in) panel pin through the side into each dowel]67[.

Repeat for the other ladder (and any intermediate ones) and complete them by sanding the sides and, if desired, painting them.

Assembling the finished shelving

If cross-bracing is to be used]68[, it is necessary only to screw the top and bottom shelves to the ladders. Drill clearance holes (Appendix 4) in the rungs which are to carry the top and bottom shelves. Screw the shelves in place]69[, then fit the cross-bracing using glue and screws.

Once the bracing is fixed you will be surprised at the increased stability of what was (probably) a wobbly assembly!

Trim the ends of the bracing, and then you can add the intermediate shelves, pinning them in position if required.

If cross-bracing is not required it will be necessary to drill *all* the rungs with clearance holes (Appendix 4), screwing *all* the shelves into place.

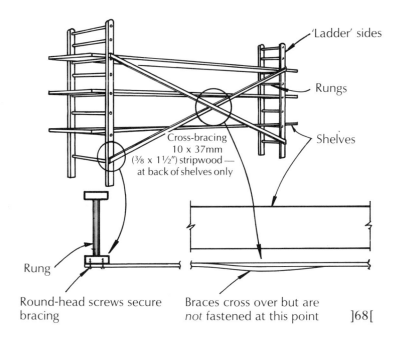

'Ladder' sides

Rungs

Shelves

Cross-bracing
10 x 37mm
(3/8 x 1½") stripwood —
at back of shelves only

Rung

Round-head screws secure
bracing

Braces cross over but are
not fastened at this point

]68[

Securing the shelf

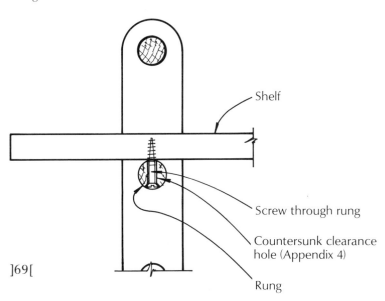

Shelf

Screw through rung

Countersunk clearance
hole (Appendix 4)

]69[

Rung

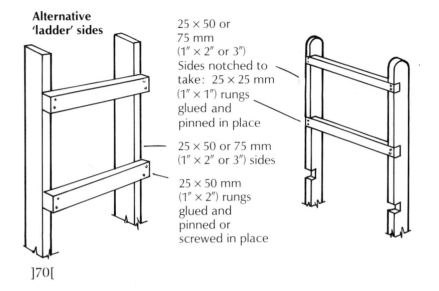

Alternative 'ladder' sides

25 × 50 or 75 mm (1" × 2" or 3") Sides notched to take: 25 × 25 mm (1" × 1") rungs glued and pinned in place

25 × 50 or 75 mm (1" × 2" or 3") sides

25 × 50 mm (1" × 2") rungs glued and pinned or screwed in place

]70[

Alternative ladder sides

Sketch]70[shows alternative ladder arrangements. The first design uses cross-supports to replace the dowels, and while it isn't nearly as neat, it saves drilling holes. The second alternative is a tidier version of the first, but it *does* call for slightly more woodworking skill in notching the uprights to take the cross-supports.

Further ideas for shelving

Many of these suggestions can be developed by combining them with the ideas on pages 30 and 44.

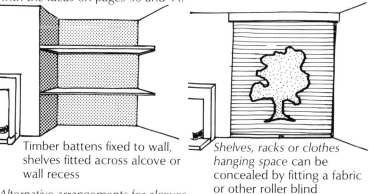

Timber battens fixed to wall, shelves fitted across alcove or wall recess

Shelves, racks or clothes *hanging space* can be concealed by fitting a fabric or other roller blind

Alternative arrangements for alcoves
Using combinations of purpose- and ready-made containers

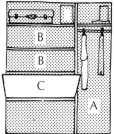

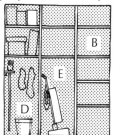

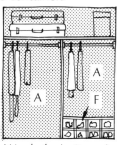

Wardrobe/ dressing-table arrangement, ideal for a bedsit. Provides hanging space (A), general storage (B) and a drop-down lid (C) for a dressing table

Cleaning/household materials storage: general storage (B), brushes and pails (D) and vacuum cleaner 'park' (E)

Wardrobe/suitcase/ shoes storage (F)

Alternative shoes storage can be made using suitable card or fibre tubes

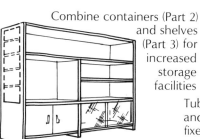

Combine containers (Part 2) and shelves (Part 3) for increased storage facilities

Tubes cut to length and glued to back panel—in turn fixed to back of storage space

Appendix 1
Tools and equipment

If you're working on a slender budget, one area in which it is advisable *not* to economise is in the selection and purchase of tools. If you use them sensibly and carefully, and store them properly when not in use, good tools will last a lifetime—or longer!

When buying tools, avoid the cheap carded tools that find their way into the scatterbins in supermarkets. Bargain-price tools are best avoided. Cheap 'edge' tools—ones with cutting edges such as chisels—blunt easily, while other tools can bend or break and can damage your work, or much more seriously, injure someone. Try to buy tools at an old-established toolshop where you will usually have the immeasurable advantage of being able to talk to someone who knows his subject.

In the following pages basic tools are illustrated, and short notes advise on their use and care. Obviously not all the tools shown are essential, but having them will make many tasks easier.

TOOLS FOR CUTTING

Saws for wood

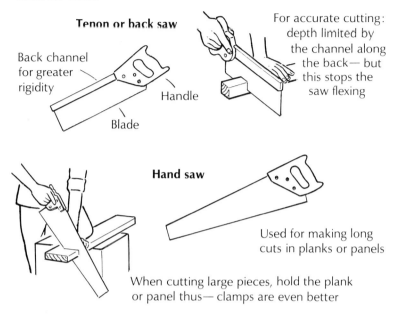

Tenon or back saw

Back channel for greater rigidity

Handle

Blade

For accurate cutting: depth limited by the channel along the back— but this stops the saw flexing

Hand saw

Used for making long cuts in planks or panels

When cutting large pieces, hold the plank or panel thus— clamps are even better

Both the saws shown above make straight cuts; for curves use the coping saw

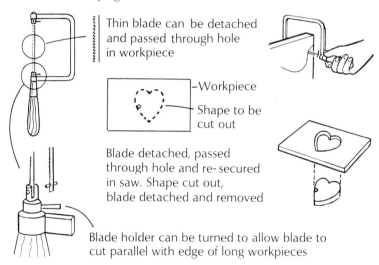

Thin blade can be detached and passed through hole in workpiece

Workpiece

Shape to be cut out

Blade detached, passed through hole and re-secured in saw. Shape cut out, blade detached and removed

Blade holder can be turned to allow blade to cut parallel with edge of long workpieces

Saws for metal

Have much finer teeth than wood saws, and are
generally made of harder metal

'Junior' hacksaw

Teeth 'point'
away from handle

Pins to
secure blade

Useful for lightweight
cutting jobs

Hacksaw

Can be adjusted
to take blades
of varying length

'Fly' nut to
tighten blade

Deeper blade
for greater
strength

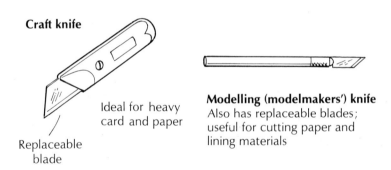

OTHER CUTTING TOOLS

Craft knife

Ideal for heavy
card and paper

Replaceable
blade

Modelling (modelmakers') knife
Also has replaceable blades;
useful for cutting paper and
lining materials

Hand drill

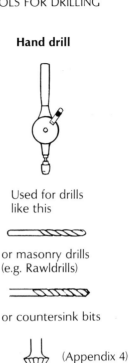

Used for drills like this

or masonry drills (e.g. Rawldrills)

or countersink bits

(Appendix 4)

Hand brace

Takes drills like this

Countersink (Appendix 4)

Screwdriver 'bit' Very useful for driving large screws

Awl
For marking out and making 'starter' holes for nails

Bradawl
For making a hole the same size as the cutting edge

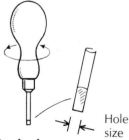

Hole size

TOOLS FOR SHAPING/SMOOTHING

Chisel

Wooden Mallet

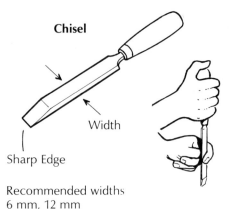

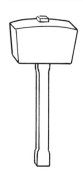

Width

Sharp Edge

Recommended widths
6 mm, 12 mm

If you *must* use blows on
a chisel use a mallet.
Relatively inexpensive,
made of boxwood, ideal for
dismantling boxes, where
the metal of a hammer
would mark the wood

Block Plane

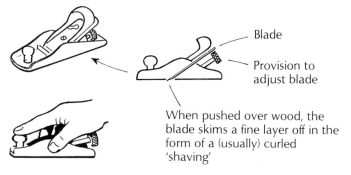

Blade

Provision to
adjust blade

When pushed over wood, the
blade skims a fine layer off in the
form of a (usually) curled
'shaving'

Sanding Block

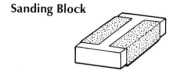

Simplest—A block of
wood with glasspaper
wrapped around it

Cork blocks, and others which hold
or secure the glasspaper, can also
be obtained

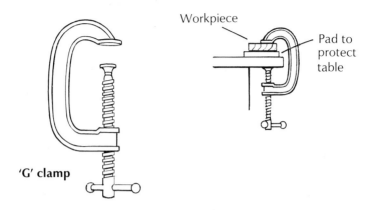

Workpiece

Pad to
protect
table

'G' clamp

Used to hold workpiece
firmly on table or bench

or to hold pieces together
while gluing or fixing

Wood scraps to protect
workpiece from clamp
marks

Pieces being
glued or screwed
together

Cross-pein

Claw hammer
For driving nails.
Claw used to
remove nails
Recommended size
20 oz (567 gr) headweight

Lightweight hammer
(sometimes called
'telephone') with
cross-pein.
Useful for
lightweight
pinning
Recommended size
3 ½ oz (99 gr)
headweight

Cross-pein hammer)
(also called
'Warrington')
For driving
nails. Useful
for starting
small nails and
pins in
confined
spaces
Recommended size
8 oz (226 gr)
headweight

Use of nailset
and hammer

Nailset
Used to drive
the heads of
small nails,
veneer and
panel pins
below the
surface

As driven
by hammer

Surface

Pin

Nailset placed
on pin/nail
head and hit
with hammer

Hole can be
filled in

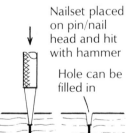

Pin

SCREWDRIVERS

Available in a wide variety of sizes, handle shapes and 'blade' widths. The following designs and sizes will be found very useful:

Blade length 100 mm (4")   Tip width 6 mm (¼")

Blade length 150 or 200 mm (6" or 8")   Tip width 4 mm ($\frac{1}{8}$")

'Stubby' or 'Dumpy' for awkward areas

Blade tip should ideally be the same width as screw slot

Appendix 2
Measurements, squareness and marking out

Measurements

Always use a flexible steel tape-measure, a metre-stick or a folding rule when taking, or marking out, measurements. Although you may have one handy, a dressmaker's fabric tape measure should be avoided; it is almost certain to be unreliable for accurate measurement owing to stretch or shrinkage.

Reading metric measurements

The metric side of the tape is usually marked out in millimetres (mm) or centimetres (cm), with each centimetre mark identified by large figures. There are 10 millimetres in a centimetre, so that if, for instance, you wanted to measure off 130 mm, you'd find the 13 cm mark (that is 130 divided by 10). If the required measurement was 137 mm, you'd still divide by 10 to find the 13 cm mark and count the last seven units (millimetres) beyond, so giving you a measurement of 137 mm.

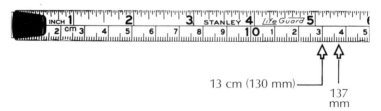

13 cm (130 mm)

137 mm

Most flexible steel tapes carry measurements in both Imperial and metric units. While it is almost always essential to stick to the units of one system or the other when measuring or marking out any given job, the tape itself can be used to convert Imperial to metric units and vice versa. This is done by unreeling the tape so that the approximate 'known' measurement is visible, and then simply reading across from one side to the other.

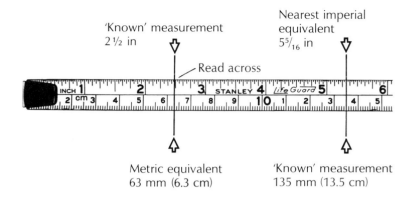

'Known' measurement 2½ in

Read across

Nearest imperial equivalent 5⁵/₁₆ in

Metric equivalent 63 mm (6.3 cm)

'Known' measurement 135 mm (13.5 cm)

Squareness

Squareness has very little to do with a square and, confusingly, something is said to be 'square with' something else when the first is exactly at right angles, or 90 degrees, to the second. The try square is the tool most often used in woodworking to test and mark squareness.

It's important that corners, or cut ends of wood and joints generally, are square. If a box or cabinet looks like this:

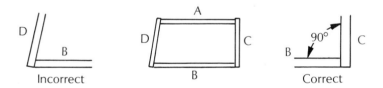

Incorrect

Correct

there are almost certainly at least two reasons for it.
1. A and B should have been the same length, but aren't!
2. The ends of A and B weren't square with D.

This illustrates the importance of accurately marking — and cutting — square ends. A little time spent on such details can save a lot of money on wasted materials.

Try square

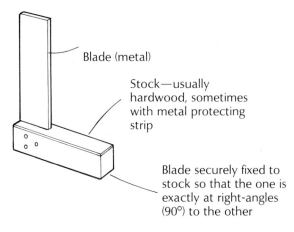

Blade (metal)

Stock—usually hardwood, sometimes with metal protecting strip

Blade securely fixed to stock so that the one is exactly at right-angles (90°) to the other

Using the try square

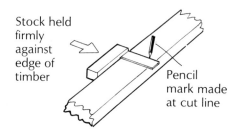

Stock held firmly against edge of timber

Pencil mark made at cut line

For marking right-angle cut lines on timber

For testing 'squareness'

Outside   or   inside

Marking out

For most purposes an HB or B grade pencil, kept sharpened to a good point, will do for marking out. When making a pencil mark against a straight edge, or any other object that has thickness, hold the pencil so that it rests firmly against the edge. In this way you'll get an accurate line.

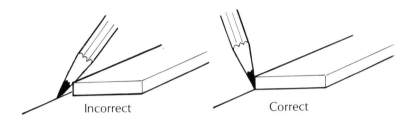

Incorrect   Correct

Circles and curves

If you have an old school compass you are admirably equipped to draw circles up to about 150 mm (6 in) in diameter. For larger circles you can simply draw around a circular object of the required size (dinner plate or tea tray?) or use the device shown below:

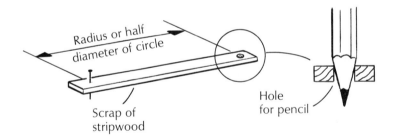

Radius or half diameter of circle

Scrap of stripwood

Hole for pencil

Stick the panel-pin point into the centre of the circle, and the pencil into the hole. Keeping the pin in place, and upright, swing the pencil end of the strip around, so drawing a circle.

Spirit level

Although really a tool, this device is included here because its main purpose is to check that shelves, cupboards, etc, are truly horizontal or vertical.

Spirit levels are
available with

wooden or

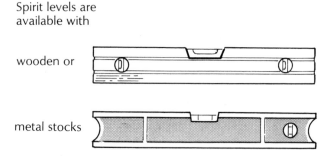

metal stocks

The recommended stock length for general household use is 600 mm (24 in).

The working element in a spirit level is a small glass or plastic vial, almost filled with tinted liquid. Each vial is accurately pre-positioned and fixed in the stock in such a way that the air bubble in the vial rests between two marks when the stock is either horizontal or vertical. By placing the stock on a shelf, for example, there is instant indication that the shelf is horizontal. If it is not, adjustment can be made until the position of the bubble indicates that the shelf *is* level.

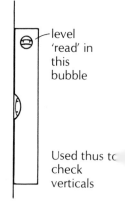

level 'read' in this bubble

Used thus tc check verticals

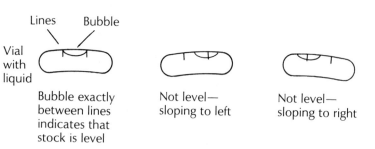

Lines   Bubble

Vial with liquid

Bubble exactly between lines indicates that stock is level

Not level— sloping to left

Not level— sloping to right

Appendix 3
Wood, panelling and boards

The wood recommended for use in this book falls into two broad categories: stripwood and softwood; and panelling.

Stripwood and softwood

Usually untreated wood cut to standard sizes, and generally available ready planed so that it is reasonably smooth to handle, and only requires the minimum of planing and/or sandpapering.

Length varies, but is generally no greater than 3900 mm (156 in) and usually about 1830 or 2440 mm (72 in or 96 in) when displayed in racks at the timber merchant. Width and thickness usually conform to standard measurements and while you can have the wood cut and finished to non-standard sizes, for economy alone it is worth asking your timber merchant for *his* list of standard sizes and using these where possible.

One of several peculiarities of the timber trade is the convention whereby softwood sizes are quoted as those for the wood *after* it was cut and *before* it was planed to a smooth surface. In other words, if you ask for 25 mm (1 in) square stripwood—and it happens to be softwood—it will in fact be 20 mm ($\frac{5}{8}$ in) square when you get it! If, on the other hand, you ask for 25 mm (1 in) square hardwood strip, it will be 25 mm (1 in) square. The only safe way around this quaint convention is to specify *always* the finished size!

Because wood is seldom available in widths greater than 250 mm (10 in) wider panels are 'manufactured', giving rise to the second broad category.

Panelling

Generally made up of sheets of very thin wood, glued together, as in plywood, or stripwood glued between thin plywood, as in 'blockboard'.

Also in large sheets, but using a different manufacturing technique, we have hardboard and chipboard.

The characteristics and uses of these materials vary, so the following notes will help in selection and identification:

Plywood

Layers of very thin wood bonded together with adhesive, with the grain of respective pieces running at right angles to one another. This arrangement makes for great strength. Can be obtained with one or both surfaces covered in a decorative wood, for example, mahogany or walnut. Available in 2440 by 1220 mm (96 by 48 in) sheets, in the following range of thicknesses:

1, 2, 4, 5, 6, 10, 12, 16 and 20 mm ($\frac{1}{16}$, $\frac{1}{8}$, $\frac{3}{16}$, $\frac{1}{4}$, $\frac{3}{8}$, $\frac{1}{2}$, $\frac{5}{8}$, $\frac{13}{16}$($\frac{3}{4}$) in)

Birch-faced plywood is recommended for the projects in this book which call for plywood.

Direction of grain

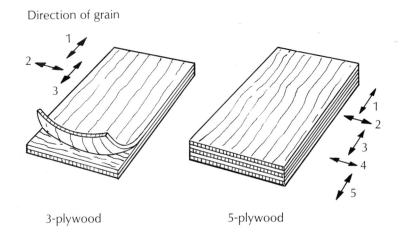

3-plywood   5-plywood

Blockboard

This consists of a sandwich of softwood strips glued between two layers of plywood. The stripwood gives strength, while the plywood ensures a smooth, flat finish. Available in sheets 2440 × 1220 mm (96 × 48 in) and larger, thickness is generally 12, 20 and 25 mm ($\frac{1}{2}$, $\frac{3}{4}$ and 1 in).

84

Blockboard

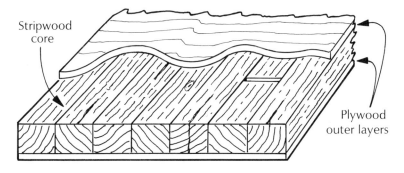

Stripwood core

Plywood outer layers

Chipboard

This is, in effect, reconstituted wood. Woodchips are compressed with a resin-bonding agent into slabs. Chipboard (also called 'particle' board) has little or nothing of the strength of timber, plywood, or blockboard, but it doesn't splinter, and takes a paint finish very well. It is difficult to glue, nail or screw successfully, and special corner connector blocks are available to help (see pp. 39, 58). Chipboard should not be used in areas subject to damp because in extreme cases moisture will cause individual wood particles to swell, distorting the bonding agent. This swelling and distortion is irreversible.

Chipboard is available in 3050 and 2440 × 1220 mm (120 and 96 × 48 in) sheets, in 12, 15, 18 and 25 mm ($\frac{1}{2}$, $\frac{5}{8}$, $\frac{3}{4}$ and 1 in) thickness. It is probably the cheapest of the thicker panelling materials, particularly when purchased in large sheets. Cutting the sheets to smaller, manageable sizes is, however, tedious.

Enterprising manufacturers were quick to recognise that homeworkers didn't want big panels, and began to offer convenient 'cut' sizes, with the very real benefit of a securely fixed veneer or melamine-type plastic coating on both faces, the 'long' edges, and for certain shelf sizes coating also on the 'short' edges. Such panels (of which Contiboard is an example) save a tremendous amount of time, particularly in finishing and painting. Obtain a list of the standard sizes which are available from your supplier. By designing within the range of widths and lengths available, virtually no time need be wasted on edge preparation.

Inevitably it becomes necessary to cut the panels at some point. Several manufacturers have devised 'iron-on' plastic edging—long strips of thin plastic, one side coated with glue, which can be cut with scissors or a sharp knife. The strip is placed in position on the edge to be covered, and a hot iron is rubbed gently over it. This melts the glue, and keeps the strip in position.

Hardboard

This is the other panelling material which, because of its (relatively) low cost, can be considered. Most easily available in 3 and 5 mm ($\frac{1}{8}$ and $\frac{3}{16}$ in) thickness and sheets 2440×1220 mm (96×48 in), hardboard has one very smooth side, while the other side has a rough textured surface.

Apart from reinforcing or lining cardboard boxes, there are very few home storage projects which would allow the use of hardboard without a supporting framework and battens, the cost of which, in materials alone, would probably outweigh any benefit from the low cost of the material itself. Also, the textured surface could prove to be a problem where blankets or woollen garments are likely to come into contact with it.

Appendix 4
Screws and nails

There is a bewildering range of screws, nails and other means for joining together wood and related materials or components. In this Appendix information is limited to the items, and sizes, most likely to be needed for simple storage systems. For example, round wire nails are available in a range of lengths between 20 mm and 200 mm ($\frac{3}{4}$ and 8 in) but the biggest you are likely to need is 75 mm (3 in). Anything longer moves into the league of carpentry and building work, and apart from requiring a very heavy hammer to drive it, it is almost certain to split any timber you are likely to encounter.

Screws and screwheads

Once again, a wide range is available, but we will concentrate on the more suitable sorts for the type of work described in this book.

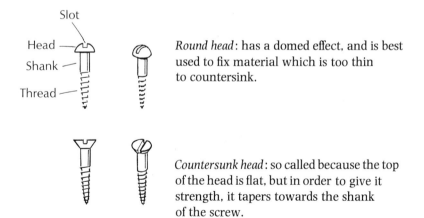

Slot

Head

Shank

Thread

Round head: has a domed effect, and is best used to fix material which is too thin to countersink.

Countersunk head: so called because the top of the head is flat, but in order to give it strength, it tapers towards the shank of the screw.

87

Cross head: also known as 'Posidriv' and 'Philips' head screws. These require a special screwdriver (Appendix 1).

 Double spiral: designed especially for use on chipboard these generally provide more secure fastenings.

TYPICAL SCREW INSTALLATIONS

Round head screw

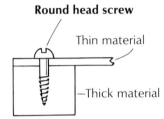

Thin material

—Thick material

Countersunk head screw

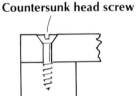

Holes for these screws must be countersunk

Metal screwcups

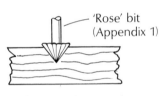

'Rose' bit (Appendix 1)

Alternatively, they can be counter-bored and filled with a plug or plaster filler

Domed cover —

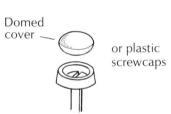

or plastic screwcaps

enable you to use countersunk screws on thin material, or obviate countersinking thick material, and also to conceal the screwheads

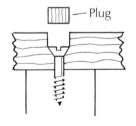

— Plug

It is very important that the correct holes are pre-drilled for screws. Failure to do so can result in splitting one or both pieces of wood, or the screw jamming so firmly that it is immovable.

There should be three drilling operations for each countersink screw:
1. Pilot hole—passes right through both pieces of material to be joined.
2. Clearance hole—passes through the upper piece of material only.
3. Countersink—or counterbore.

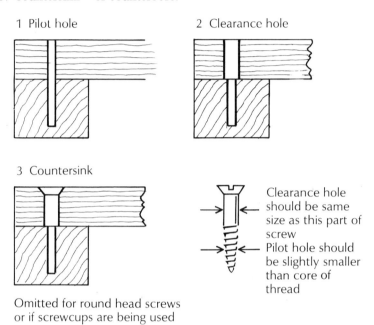

1 Pilot hole   2 Clearance hole

3 Countersink

Clearance hole should be same size as this part of screw

Pilot hole should be slightly smaller than core of thread

Omitted for round head screws or if screwcups are being used

When possible, adhesive (Appendix 5) should be used in conjunction with nails and screws.

Selecting the length

Ideally, the screw should be long enough to pass three-quarters of the distance into the material to which it is being fixed:

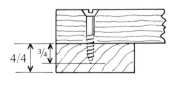

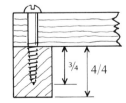

NAILS

Round wire	Oval wire	Panel pins	Veneer pins
For heavier construction work—large head is ugly and hard to conceal	For joints in relatively heavy timber— should be driven with long part of oval parallel with grain Head can be driven below surface using nailset (Appendix 1)	For lighter/cabinet work Head can be driven below surface using nailset	
Lengths 20 to 75 mm ($\frac{3}{4}''$ to 3")	Lengths 25 to 75 mm (1" to 3 ")	Lengths 10, 20, 25, 40 mm ($\frac{3}{8}''$, $\frac{3}{4}''$, 1", $1\frac{1}{2}''$)	Lengths 10, 20 mm ($\frac{3}{8}''$, $\frac{3}{4}''$)
Recommended 25, 50 (1", 2")	*Recommended 25, 50 mm (1" to 2 ")*	*Selection recommended*	*Both recommended*

Appendix 5
Adhesives

There are dozens of adhesives available, many of them very expensive and very specialised. For the projects described in this book, however, there are three adhesives which will serve most purposes and, once acquired, will be found useful for many other gluing jobs.

The information given below is for guidance only. When gluing fabrics, plastics and the like, *always* test the adhesive on scraps of *both* materials to be joined. If colours don't run, or plastics haven't begun to melt or blister by the time the test piece has dried (usually when the strong smell has disappeared), it's fairly safe to proceed.

When applying adhesives *always* follow the instructions on the container, particularly with regard to surface preparation and safety. If the manufacturer says that the product should be used in a well-ventilated area, he means it!

For joining	Use
Wood to wood	White PVA (eg Evode Resin W)
Card or fibre to wood	White PVA
Card or fibre to card or fibre	White PVA
Paper to card, fibre or wood	Wallpaper paste (eg Polycell)
Fabric to card, fibre or wood	Latex (eg Copydex)
Expanded vinyl to anything	Refer to manufacturer's instructions
Coated chipboard to wood or to coated chipboard	Follow manufacturer's recommendations if available. If not, a contact adhesive (eg Thixofix) is generally effective.

Appendix 6
Painting and finishing

Painting or otherwise finishing the projects described in this book follows a fairly clear sequence: preparation, priming (or undercoating) and then coating.

Preparation

Whatever you're going to paint, or coat, is almost certain to require some preparation. All materials should be dry and free from dust or oil substances. Holes, gaps and other blemishes should be filled with 'Polyfilla' type plasters or with plastic wood—both should be thoroughly dry before sandpapering. Wood should be sandpapered to a smooth finish, using progressively finer grades of sandpaper and then glasspaper.

Priming or undercoating

In porous materials the purpose of this stage is to seal the pores, in effect filling them with the primer or undercoat; this is partly to stop the material soaking up the final finish, and partly to help smooth the surface. Cardboard and fibre can be primed quite effectively by brushing inside and out with ordinary wallpaper adhesive. Follow the manufacturer's instructions—preferably using a thinner mix than you would for paperhanging. This mix is almost always identified in the instructions as 'size' or 'wall size'.

Wood—including blockboard and plywood—which is to be painted should be primed with a substance compatible with the paint you plan to use for the final finish. Emulsion-based paints can be thinned with ordinary tap water to make an inexpensive primer or undercoat. Priming a surface which is to be varnished is best done using varnish slightly diluted with the recommended solvent. After sandpapering, apply a first coat of primer, and when it is thoroughly dry, rub the surface down with very fine glasspaper. If you want a super-smooth finish, repeat this operation; if not, wipe the surfaces thoroughly. Then go on to the next stage.

Coating

This can be done with paint or varnish. Make sure the paint (or varnish) is thoroughly stirred, then dip the brush into the paint until half the length of the bristles is covered. This is known as 'charging' the brush. Wipe excess paint off on the inside edge of the can, then begin painting by using gentle, even strokes in one direction—usually along the length of the object. Try to achieve a coating of uniform thickness. With light falling the right way you can usually see thick areas or 'runs' and these can be 'eased' out by painting over them—again moving the brush in one direction.

When this coat is dry, you may feel quite satisfied and decide to stop there. Purists would almost certainly want to rub the coat down with fine glasspaper, then apply a final coat.

Choosing paint

There are two basic types of paint available for domestic use: emulsion-based or oil-based. Emulsion-based paints are water soluble, which means that you can wash your brushes in cold water.

Oil-based paints and varnishes are characterised by their glossy finish when dry; by the fact that objects finished in them can be easily washed when soiled or grubby; and by their solvent, which is generally pure turpentine or turpentine substitute. Paints are opaque, therefore conceal what is beneath them: varnishes are transparent.

When buying the relatively small quantities of paint or varnish needed for the storage systems described in this book, read the instructions on the tin. These should tell you how many square metres the paint will cover, and what substance to use to clean brushes, rollers and any nasty blodges on the carpet. If the substance is anything other than water, buy some at the same time—you'll need it to clean your paintbrush.

Paintbrushes

The advice given in Appendix 1 about the choice and care of tools applies equally to the choice and care of brushes. Initially you're unlikely to need more than two sizes, perhaps 20 mm and 50 mm ($\frac{3}{4}$ and 2 in) wide. Use the smaller one for edges, corners and fine work, and the wider one for broad surfaces.

Cleaning brushes

Always clean your brushes after use. This is not a particularly exciting task and is one which we tend to defer until it's too late. Result—the purchase of new brushes when we next have a painting job on our hands!

Wipe as much surplus paint as possible on to a rag or newspaper. Place some of the solvent in a container—plastic if the solvent is water, metal (an empty baked bean can will do) if it's white spirit or turpentine substitute or one of the smelly substances. Slosh the brush about in the solvent, *gently* flexing the bristles to work the solvent high into them. When the bristles look reasonably clear of paint, hold the brush under running water, so washing out most of the remaining paint and solvent. Now add a biggish squirt of domestic washing-up liquid to the bristles, and work this in, easing the bristles apart with your fingers and, in so doing, freeing the last of the paint and solvent. The washing-up liquid will probably turn into a thickish foam, tinted with whatever colour you have been using. Hold the brush under running water again, and ease all the foam out. By now the bristles should be quite clean. Use a cloth to absorb excess moisture, then wrap the bristle part of the brush in a little 'parcel' as shown—and store it in a reasonably dry place.

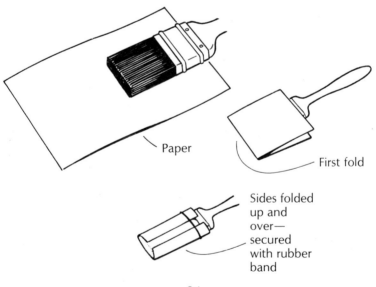

Paper

First fold

Sides folded up and over— secured with rubber band

Painted decoration

Tea chests and some of the other containers described earlier in this book can be quite attractively painted—simply or, if skill permits, in elaborate styles similar to British traditional long-boat or perhaps Romany caravan decoration. Both styles are an art form which, if taken seriously, calls for a lot of study and research, to say nothing of time, skill and large numbers of small pots of paint. For present purposes we'll confine ourselves to the fairly simple decoration of a tea chest. We'll assume that the chest has been painted in scarlet gloss paint, with the metal edging 'picked out' in black gloss paint.

Suppose you have decided to decorate each of the four sides of the box with a single large sunflower. Using tracing paper, brown wrapping paper, or even newspaper, lay out the design to full size, using a felt-tip marker pen, a crayon, or soft pencil. If the design is one calling for symmetry around the centre of each panel you can lay out only half the design, then turn it over, or crease the paper down the middle, and cut out the flower petals and centre. The result will be a paper pattern of the sunflower, cut out stencil-fashion.

There are now two ways you can proceed. Either place the paper pattern in position and, following the cutout, draw the sunflower on the

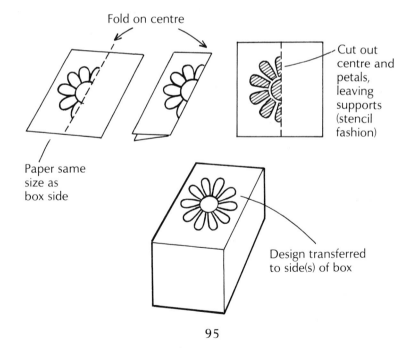

Fold on centre

Cut out centre and petals, leaving supports (stencil fashion)

Paper same size as box side

Design transferred to side(s) of box

side of the box using a 2B or 3B pencil; or transfer the pattern on to rigid card (Bristol board about 1 mm thick is ideal—but expensive), cut it out and use it as a guide for the pencil. The latter course is strongly recommended if the pattern is to be repeated a number of times.

You now have a pencil outline of the sunflower on the side of the box. A reasonably priced squirrel-hair brush, say a No 8 or 9, purchased from an art materials shop (avoid the brushes sold on toy counters or provided in children's paint-boxes!) is used to paint in the petals a bright yellow. If possible use the same sort of paint as the background finish, eg oil paint on oil paint or emulsion paint on emulsion. Carefully working within the pencil pattern, paint the outline of the petals. Keep the brush fairly well charged and have a thin stick handy to stir the paint frequently. Don't worry if the edge lines aren't perfect—from a few feet away, and when the flower is complete, blemishes will be hardly noticeable. Fill in between the outline, and when all the petals are finished, *leave the paint to dry.* Using the same technique, paint the centre of the flower in, say, mid-brown.

The possibilities of this sort of decoration are endless. The three ideas shown below will almost certainly suggest others.

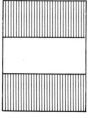
Contrasting
colour
band(s)

Same pattern
repeated

Symbols
to indicate
box content

Appendix 7
Hinges, fittings and accessories

These can be surprisingly expensive unless you're prepared to look around and compare prices. It helps to have some idea of what you require, and the illustrations on the following pages may prove useful. If cost is an important consideration, and you have the moral courage to root about in rubbish skips, or to scrounge off friends, 'throw-out' furniture can be cannibalised for useful hinges and fittings.

Whether you buy the items 'loose' or in carded display packs, check that you have screws of the correct size, not only for the hinges or fittings themselves, but also for the material to which you're fixing them.

Hinges

Of the fittings needed for projects in this book, hinges are probably the most common. Almost all doors, lids or covers for containers need hinges. In order to function correctly, hinges must be properly fitted, and while traditional hinges call for a certain amount of fitting skill, there are a number of proprietary designs on the market which are easy to fit accurately.

In this Appendix guidance is given in some detail on fitting traditional hinges, and then the newer types are illustrated. Knowledge of how to deal with old-fashioned hinges will enable you to understand the new ones quite easily.

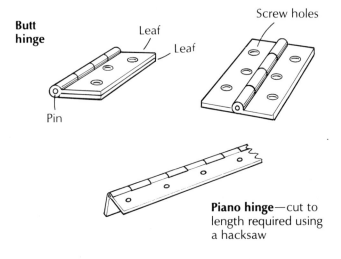

Butt hinge

Leaf

Leaf

Pin

Screw holes

Piano hinge—cut to length required using a hacksaw

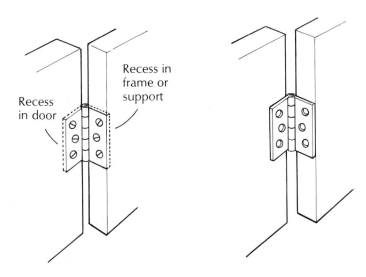

Recess in door

Recess in frame or support

Option 1

A difficult job, but giving a very tidy effect; the leaves of the hinge are recessed into the wood of both the door and the support.

Option 2

A much easier job; the recesses are omitted, but the door is held away from the frame by the thickness of both leaves of the hinge.

98

Stage 1 : marking out

This operation is similar for most types of hinge, and for both the options shown (p. 98). For our example we will assume that a hinged lid is being fitted to a tea chest.

a Decide which edge of the box is to carry the hinges

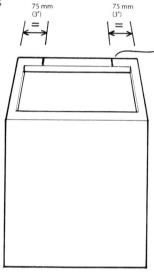

Make pencil marks the same distance in from each end (75 mm (3″) in this example)

b   Open the hinge out as far as it will go

Note that pin and round part of hinge extend over edge of frame

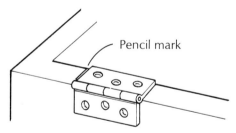

Pencil mark

c   Lay one end of one hinge leaf on the first pencil mark

Holding the hinge steady, draw around it in pencil, also marking the screw holes

Repeat for the other hinge and for any intermediate hinges

99

Stage 2 (optional): cutting recesses

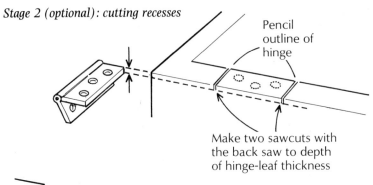

Pencil
outline of
hinge

Make two sawcuts with
the back saw to depth
of hinge-leaf thickness

Finished
effect

Use a chisel to remove the wood between the
sawcuts. The bottom of the recess should be
flat, and the hinge should fit snugly

You will, of course, have removed the pencil
marks for the screw holes—replace these by
repeating Stage 1c

Stage 3: fixing hinges

Drill pilot holes (Appendix 4) and screw the hinges into position.

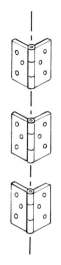

Note: When two or more hinges are
used for the same panel or door, it is
very important that all the 'pins'
should line up on the same axis, as if,
in effect, they were one long pin.

100

Stage 4: marking out the lid

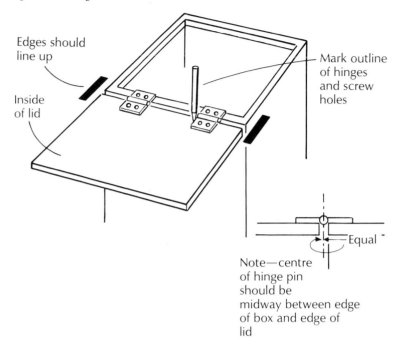

Edges should line up

Inside of lid

Mark outline of hinges and screw holes

Equal

Note—centre of hinge pin should be midway between edge of box and edge of lid

If the lid is very heavy and you find it difficult to hold and mark the lid as shown, a rearrangement of the box and lid at this stage may prove helpful.

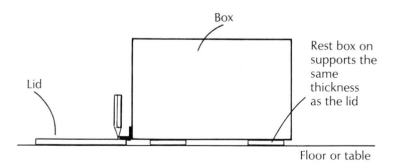

Box

Rest box on supports the same thickness as the lid

Lid

Floor or table

Stage 5 (optional): recessing the lid

Here the aim is to cut recesses in the lid, counterparts to the recesses made in the box frame. But because the lid is much wider than the frame you can't make saw-cuts, and must use a chisel to define the edges of the recesses.

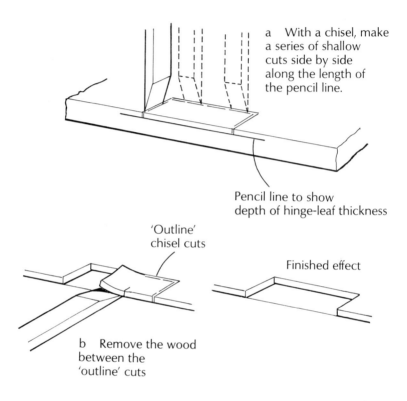

a   With a chisel, make a series of shallow cuts side by side along the length of the pencil line.

Pencil line to show depth of hinge-leaf thickness

'Outline' chisel cuts

Finished effect

b   Remove the wood between the 'outline' cuts

Stage 6: fixing hinges

This is virtually identical to Stage 3: drill holes and screw the hinges to the lid.

Easy-fix hinges

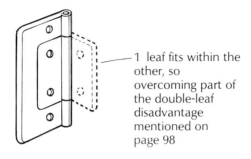

1 leaf fits within the other, so overcoming part of the double-leaf disadvantage mentioned on page 98

Concealed hinges—so called because they do not protrude beyond, and are therefore not visible outside, the box or cabinet

Cabinet side

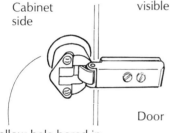

Door

Shallow hole bored in side panel to take circular part of hinge

Strongly recommended for chipboard panels

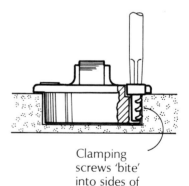

Clamping screws 'bite' into sides of hole, so securing hinge

Cupboard catches

Mainly to hold doors or lids in the closed position

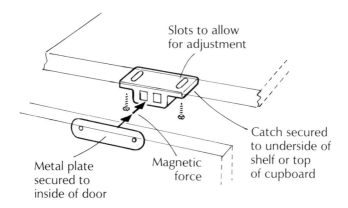

Slots to allow for adjustment

Catch secured to underside of shelf or top of cupboard

Magnetic force

Metal plate secured to inside of door

Cupboard 'buttons'

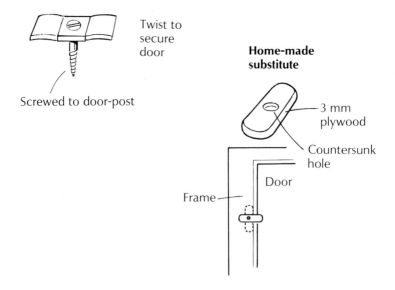

Twist to secure door

Home-made substitute

Screwed to door-post

3 mm plywood

Countersunk hole

Door

Frame

Reinforcing brackets

If joints are not as strong as you could
have wished, one or other of these
brackets may help

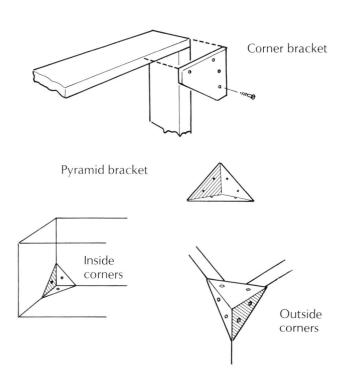

Corner bracket

Pyramid bracket

Inside
corners

Outside
corners

d and door stays

ed to prevent doors from opening too far, and to hold lift-up or drop-
wn flaps in the 'open' position. Again, many types are available, and
e manufacturer's fitting instructions should be followed.

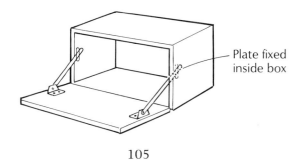

Plate fixed
inside box

Drawer pulls and cupboard knobs

These vary in design, complexity and cost, as well as in method of fitting. Simpler types are generally fixed with one or more screws passing through the door or drawer panel, from the inside, into the knob.

Where knobs or pulls of this type are fitted to card or fibre boxes, it is as well to provide a panel of hardboard or plywood reinforcement.

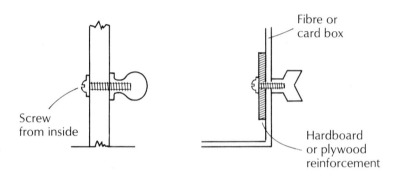

Screw from inside

Fibre or card box

Hardboard or plywood reinforcement

Mirror plates

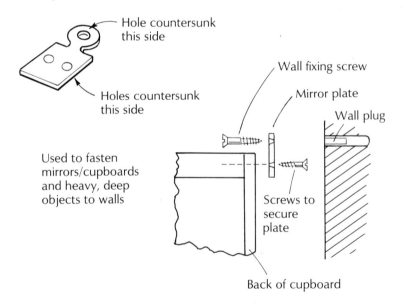

Hole countersunk this side

Holes countersunk this side

Used to fasten mirrors/cupboards and heavy, deep objects to walls

Wall fixing screw

Mirror plate

Wall plug

Screws to secure plate

Back of cupboard

Appendix 8
Wall fixings

Wall fixings range from not-very-reliable adhesive devices, such as those found on the back of plastic coat-hooks, to massive anchor-bolt arrangements which will safely hold access ladders to the sides of buildings.

For our purposes, we need something midway between the two—a method of fixing that offers simplicity, reliability and strength.

Plugs and plugging

Normally it is not possible to drive a screw straight into a brick or concrete wall. A hole somewhat larger than the screw is needed, and the hole is plugged with a substance in which the screw threads will 'bite'. The substance can be wood or one of a number of cunning proprietary plugs, all of which expand slightly as the screw is driven in, so firmly securing the screw, and whatever it is holding, to the wall.

Wooden plugs

This is the oldest, and certainly the cheapest, way to plug a wall. Cut a tapered strip of wood slightly longer than the screw, with the narrow end

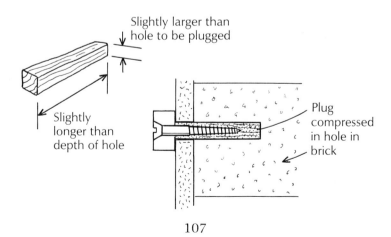

Slightly larger than hole to be plugged

Slightly longer than depth of hole

Plug compressed in hole in brick

of the taper very slightly larger than the hole. Hammer the plug into the hole until it is flush with the surface. Using a pilot-hole size drill (Appendix 4), drill into the centre of the plug to a depth roughly half the length of the screw.

Plastic (proprietary) plugs

When buying these, it is a good idea to standardise on one screw size (No 6 is recommended for any of the projects in this book) and buy a range of plugs of varying lengths for the same size of screw (very often they are colour coded). At the same time, buy a Rawldrill or tungsten-tipped masonry drill (Appendix 1) to suit.

Brick walls, concrete and masonry

The first requirement is to drill one or more holes, as accurately as possible, in the positions marked.

You can do this by using a Rawldrill and hammer. A Rawldrill is a hardened steel-fluted drill, fixed in a heavy metal handle (Appendix 1). The point is driven into the brickwork by thumping the handle with a hammer and, between each blow, turning the handle slightly. This is an inexpensive way to make holes in brickwork, but it is very slow and very tedious. A speedier, if more costly way is to use a two-speed power drill. Working on the low speed and using a special tungsten steel-tipped 'bit', you will accelerate the job wonderfully.

A word of warning—if you are drilling through plaster and then into brickwork (or stone or concrete), there's a good chance that because the plaster is relatively soft, the drill will 'creep' or deflect away from the mark on which you are drilling. To avoid this, hold the drill very firmly and once it is turning, drive it quickly through the plaster. When you feel it encounter the resistance of the brickwork, withdraw the drill, switch it off and check that the hole is, indeed, where you want it. All being well, reinsert the drill, hold it firmly against the brickwork, then switch on. Continue, forcing the drill slowly but firmly a few millimetres into the brickwork. Ease the pressure on the drill, partially withdraw it to clear the brickdust, then continue alternately drilling, a few millimetres at a time, and withdrawing, until the hole is the required depth.

If, after making the initial hole through the plaster, you find that the drill has, in fact, crept or deflected, re-drill, slanting the drill point slightly to correct the deflection. When the drill point reaches the brick, pause, then move the drill away from the slant and back to the correct right-angles-to-the-wall drilling position. Switch off, check, and then proceed as already described.

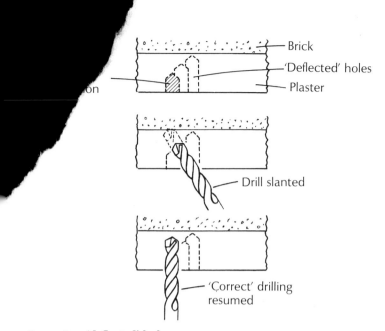

Brick
'Deflected' holes
Plaster

Drill slanted

'Correct' drilling
resumed

Correcting 'deflected' holes

Insert the selected plugs and drive the fixing screw part way in. Unscrew it, then repeat, this time passing the screw through the bracket, or panel, or whatever is to be screwed to the wall. Drive the screw right home, giving it a few final turns to make it as tight as possible.

Hollow walls

It is not a good idea to hang very heavy shelves or cabinets on hollow walls. For lighter objects, however, several proprietary devices are made, and the manufacturer's instructions should be carefully followed. Three such proprietary devices are shown (page 110). An understanding of how they work will help you to discuss the variations available with your hardware merchant.

Masonry nails

These are hardened steel nails which can be used to fix battens and stripwood to walls. They should *not* be used to secure shelves or anything which projects sufficiently from the wall to create an outward 'pulling' effect. Masonry nails can be quite dangerous to use—they must always be driven with an engineer's hardened steel hammer, and because they can shatter as they are being driven, you should wear plastic safety goggles. *Not* recommended for beginners.

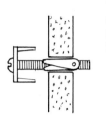

Toggles fold over screw to pass through hole

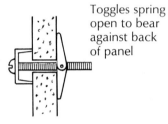

Toggles spring open to bear against back of panel

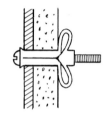

Spring toggle

Collapsible toggle

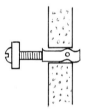

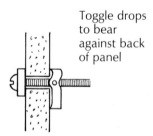

Toggle drops to bear against back of panel

Gravity toggle

Appendix 9

Storage box seating

Padded tops for storage containers which also serve as seats are very easily made.

For our simple seating we assume a wooden base of some sort, in all probability fitted with a sub-base which keeps the lid or cover in place on the storage container.

Our main aim is to cover the top surface of the wooden base with padding, secure the padding in place, and then cover it with a material that is both attractive and hard wearing.

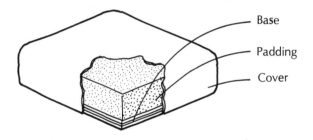

Base
Padding
Cover

Padding

For our purposes the simplest to use and most easily available padding is rubber (latex) or plastic (polyether) foam. Rubber foam is tougher, longer lasting and generally more resilient than plastic. It is also more expensive. Foams are available in blocks and sheets of varying sizes, and can be cut to size using scissors, a craft knife or, for thicker pieces, a finely serrated kitchen knife.

Warning: Some foams are both inflammable and – worse – once alight emit highly toxic fumes. Make sure you know what you are buying . . . and *take due care.*

Covering

Here you can use conventional upholstery fabrics, and
not going to need very big pieces, the cost can be quite
more so if colour or pattern match isn't important, and yo
with some of the bargains to be found in the 'remnants
supplying furnishing fabric.

An alternative to fabric is the use of expanded vinyl leathe
looks and feels like leather, is easy to work with, and ha
advantages: if it gets dirty it can be cleaned using a cloth and
soapy water. Unlike fabrics, the cut edges won't fray and need no
attention.

Sewing

Whether fabric or expanded vinyl leathercloth is used, some sewing is
desirable—but by no means essential. If a sewing machine is available,
use the heaviest gauge needle you can, and the strongest thread. The
same applies to hand-sewing—for our relatively simple upholstered
shapes, exotic equipment like curved needles and 'sailmaker's palms' isn't
necessary. If sewing of any sort is beyond you, you can dispense with it
entirely by gluing the edges of the fabric together, or by arranging the
expanded vinyl material so that 'corners' fold out of sight.

The following sequence shows the stages in covering a padded top for a
square box. Circular tops are covered along similar lines.

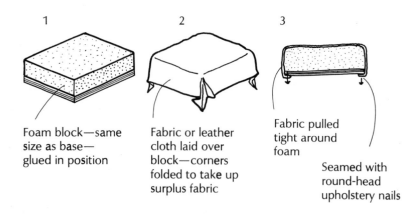

1

Foam block—same
size as base—
glued in position

2

Fabric or leather
cloth laid over
block—corners
folded to take up
surplus fabric

3

Fabric pulled
tight around
foam

Seamed with
round-head
upholstery nails